BLACK LEGACY PRESS™
WWW.BLACKLEGACYPRESS.ORG

SLAVE NARRATIVES

VOLUME XVI
TEXAS NARRATIVES
PART 4

By
United States.
Work Projects Administration

Copyright © 2024 by BLACKLEGACYPRESS.ORG

All rights reserved. No part of this publication may be reproduced or transmitted in any form or by any means electronic or mechanical, including information storage and retrieval systems without permission in writing from the publisher, except for student research using the appropriate citations.

ISBN: 978-1-63652-208-1

SLAVE NARRATIVES

A Folk History of Slavery in the United States.
From Interviews with Former Slaves

**UNITED STATES.
WORK PROJECTS ADMINISTRATION**

TYPEWRITTEN RECORDS PREPARED BY
THE FEDERAL WRITERS' PROJECT
1936-1938
ASSEMBLED BY
THE LIBRARY OF CONGRESS PROJECT
WORK PROJECTS ADMINISTRATION
FOR THE DISTRICT OF COLUMBIA
SPONSORED BY THE LIBRARY OF
CONGRESS

WASHINGTON 1941

VOLUME XVI
TEXAS NARRATIVES
PART 4

Prepared by
The Federal Writers' Project of
The Works Progress Administration
For the State of Texas

CONTENTS

Mazique Sanco 1
Clarissa Scales 5
Hannah Scott 9
Abram Sells 13
George Selman 21
Callie Shepherd 25
Betty Simmons 29
George Simmons 35
Ben Simpson 39
Giles Smith 43
James W. Smith 49
Jordon Smith 55
Millie Ann Smith 63
Susan Smith 69
John Sneed 73
Mariah Snyder 81
Patsy Southwell 85
Leithean Spinks 87
Guy Stewart 93
William Stone 97
Yach Stringfellow 103
Bert Strong 107
Emma Taylor 113
Mollie Taylor 119

Jake Terriell	121
J.W. Terrill	123
Allen Thomas	127
Bill and Ellen Thomas	131
Lucy Thomas	137
Philles Thomas	141
William M. Thomas	147
Mary Thompson	153
Penny Thompson	157
Albert Todd	163
Aleck Trimble	167
Reeves Tucker	175
Lou Turner	179
Irella Battle Walker	185
John Walton	189
Sol Walton	193
Ella Washington	199
Rosa Washington	203
Sam Jones Washington	209
William Watkins	215
Dianah Watson	219
Emma Watson	223
James West	227
Adeline White	233
Sylvester SostanWickliffe	237
Daphne Williams	243
Horatio W. Williams	249

Lou Williams	253
Millie Williams	261
Rose Williams	267
Steve Williams	273
Wayman Williams	277
Willie Williams	285
Lulu Wilson	291
Wash Wilson	299
Willis Winn	307
Rube Witt	315
Ruben Woods	321
Willis Woodson	325
James G. Woorling	329
Caroline Wright	333
Sallie Wroe	337
Fannie Yarbrough	341
Litt Young	345
Louis Young	351
Teshan Young	355

MAZIQUE SANCO

Mazique Sanco was born a slave of Mrs. Louisa Green, in Columbia, South Carolina, on February 10, 1849. Shortly after Mazique was freed, he enlisted in the army and was sent with the Tenth Cavalry to San Angelo, then Fort Concho, Texas. After Mazique left the army he became well-known as a chef, and worked for several large hotels. Mazique uses little dialect. When asked where Mazique is, his young wife says, "In his office," and upon inquiry as to the location of this office, she replies mirthfully, "On de river," for since he is too old to work, Mazique spends most of his time fishing.

"My mistress owned a beautiful home and three hundred twenty acres of land in the edge of Columbia, in South Carolina, just back of the state house. Her name was Mrs. Louisa Green and she was a widow lady. That's where I was born, but when her nephew, Dr. Edward Flemming, married Miss Dean, I was given to him for a wedding present, and so was my mother and her other children. I was a very small boy then, and when I was ten Dr. Flemming gave me to his crippled mother-in-law for a foot boy. She got crippled in a runaway accident, when her husband was killed. He had two fine horses, fiery and spirited as could be had. He called them Ash and Dash, and one day he and his wife were out driving and the horses ran the carriage into a big pine tree, and Mr. Dean was killed instantly, and Mrs. Dean couldn't ever help herself again. I waited on her. I had a good bed and food and was let to earn ten cent shin plasters.

"When the war was over she called up her five families of slaves and told us we could go or stay. Some went and some stayed. I was always an adventurer, wanting to see and learn things, so I left and went back to my mother with Mrs. Flemming.

Mazique Sanco

"I only stayed there a few months and hired out to Major Legg, and worked for him several years. I felt I wasn't learning enough, so I joined the United States Army and with a hundred and eighty-five boys went to St. Louis, Missouri. From there we were transferred with the Tenth Cavalry to Fort Concho. I helped haul the lumber from San Antonio to finish the buildings at the fort. I was there five years.

"After I went to work at private employment I did some carpenter work, but most of the houses were adobe or pecan pole buildings, so I got a job from Mr. Jimmy Keating as mechanic for awhile, and then drifted to Mexico. Odd jobs were all I could get for awhile, so I landed in El Paso and got a job in a hotel.

"That was the start of my success, for I learned to be a skilled chef and superintended the kitchens in some of the largest hotels in Texas. I made as high as $80.00, in Houston. My last work was done at the St. Angelus Hotel here in San Angelo and if you don't believe I'm a good cook, just look at my wife over there. When I married her she was fourteen years old and weighed a hundred and fifteen pounds. Now it's been a long time since I could get her on the scales, not since she passed the two hundred pound mark."

United States. Work Projects Administration

CLARISSA SCALES

Clarissa Scales, 79, was born a slave of William Vaughan, on his plantation at Plum Creek, Texas. Clarissa married when she was fifteen. She owns a small farm near Austin, but lives with her son, Arthur, at 1812 Cedar Ave., Austin.

"Mammy's name was Mary Vaughan and she was brung from Baton Rouge, what am over in Louisiana, by our master. He went and located on Plum Creek, down in Hays County.

"Mammy was a tall, heavy-set woman, more'n six foot tall. She was a maid-doctor after freedom. Dat mean she nussed women at childbirth. She allus told me de last thing she saw when she left Baton Rouge was her mammy standin' on a big, wood block to be sold for a slave. Dat de last time she ever saw her mammy. Mammy died 'bout fifty years ago. She was livin' on a farm on Big Walnut Creek, in Travis County. Daddy done die a year befo' and she jes' grieves herself to death. Daddy was sho' funny lookin', 'cause he wore long whiskers and what you calls a goatee. He was field worker on de Vaughan plantation.

"Master Vaughan was good and treated us all right. He was a great white man and didn't have no over seer. Missy's name was Margaret, and she was good, too.

"My job was tendin' fires and herdin' hawgs. I kep'

fire goin' when de washin' bein' done. Dey had plenty wood, but used corn cobs for de fire. Dere a big hill corn cobs near de wash kettle. In de evenin' I had to bring in de hawgs. I had a li'l whoop I druv dem with, a eight-plaited rawhide whoop on de long stick. It a purty sight to see dem hawgs go under de slip-gap, what was a rail took down from de bottom de fence, so de hawgs could run under.

"Injuns used to pass our cabin in big bunches. One time dey give mammy some earrings, but when they's through eatin' they wants dem earrings back. Dat de way de Injuns done. After feedin' dem, mammy allus say, 'Be good and kind to everybody.'

"One day Master Vaughan come and say we's all free and could go and do what we wants. Daddy and mammy rents a place and I stays until I's fifteen. I wanted to be a teacher, but daddy kep' me hoein' cotton most de time. Dat's all he knowed. He allus told me it was 'nough larnin' could I jes' read and write. He never even had dat much. But he was de good farmer and good to me and mammy.

"Dere was a school after freedom. Old Man Tilden was de teacher. One time a bunch of men dey calls de Klu Klux come in de room and say, 'You git out of here and git 'way from dem niggers. Don' let us cotch you here when we comes back.' Old Man Tilden sho' was scart, but he say, 'You all come back tomorrow.' He finishes dat year and we never hears of him 'gain. Dat a log schoolhouse on Williamson Creek, five mile south of Austin.

Clarissa Scales

"Den a cullud teacher named Hamlet Campbell come down from de north. He rents a room in a big house and makes a school. De trustees hires and pays him and us chillen didn't have to pay. I got to go some, and I allus tells my granddaughter how I's head of de class when I does go. She am good in her studies, too.

"When I's fifteen I marries Benjamin Calhoun Scales and he was a farmer. We had five chillen and three boys is livin'. One am a preacher and Arthur am a cement laborer and Chester works in a printin' shop.

"Benjie dies on February 15th, dis year (1937). I lives with Arthur and de gov'ment gives me $10.00 de month. I has de li'l farm of nineteen acres out near Oak Hill and Floyd, de preacher, lives on dat. All my boys is good to me. Dey done good, and better'n we could, 'cause we couldn't git much larnin' dem days. I's had de good life. But we 'preciated our chance more'n de young folks does nowadays. Dey has so much dey don't have to try so hard. If we'd had what dey got, we'd thunk we was done died and gone to Glory Land. Maybe dey'll be all right when deys growed."

HANNAH SCOTT

Hannah Scott was born in slavery, in Alabama. She does not know her age but says she was grown when her last master, Bat Peterson, set her free. Hannah lives with her grandson in a two-room house near the railroad tracks, in Houston, Texas. Unable to walk because of a paralytic stroke, Hannah asked her grandson to lift her from the bed to a chair, from which she told her story.

"Son, move de chair a mite closer to de stove. Dere, dat's better, 'cause de heat kind of soople me up. Ain't nothin' left of me but some skin and bones, nohow.

"Lemme see now. I's born in Alabama and I think dey calls it Fayette County. Mama's name was Ardissa and she 'long to Marse Clark Eccles, but us chillen allus call him White Pa. Miss Hetty, his wife, we calls her White Ma.

"I never knowed my own pa, 'cause he 'long to 'nother man and was sold away 'fore I's old 'nough to know him. Mama has five us chillen, but dey all dead 'ceptin' me. Dey didn't have no marriage back den like now. Dey just puts black folks together in de sight of man and not in de sight of Gawd, and dey puts dem asunder, too.

"Marse Eccles didn't have no big place and only nine slaves. I guess he what you calls 'poor folks,' but he mighty good to he black folks. I 'member when he sold us to Bat Peterson. He and White Ma break down and cry when old Bat puts us in de wagon and takes us off to Arkansas. I heared mama say something 'bout White Pa sellin' us for debt and he gits a hunerd dollars for me.

"Whoosh, it sho' was a heap dif'ent from Alabama. Marse Bat had niggers. I reckon he must of had a hunerd of dem and two nigger drivers, Uncle Green and Uncle Jake, and a overseer. Marse Bat was mean, too, and work he slaves from daylight till nine o'clock at night. I carries water for de hands. I carries de bucket on my head and 'fore long I ain't got no more hair on my head den you has on de palm of you hand. No, suh!

"When I gits bigger, de overseer puts me in de field with de rest. Marse Bat grow mostly cotton and it don't make no dif'ence is you big or li'l, you better keep up or de drivers burn you up with de whip, sho' 'nough. Old Marse Bat never put a lick on me all de years I 'longs to him, but de drivers sho' burnt me plenty times. Sometime I gits so tired come night, I draps right in de row and gone to sleep. Den de driver come 'long and, wham, dey cuts you 'cross de back with de whip and you wakes up when it lights on you, yes, suh! 'Bout nine o'clock dey hollers 'cotton up' and dat de quittin' signal. We goes to de quarters and jes' drap on de bunk and go to sleep without nothin' to eat.

"On old Bat's place dat all us know, is work and more work. De onlies' time we has off am Sunday and den we has to wash and mend clothes. De first Sunday of de month a white preacher come, but all he say is 'bedience to de white folks, and we hears 'nough of dat without him tellin' us.

"I 'member when White Pa come to try git mama and us chillen back. We been in Arkansas five, six year, and, whoosh, I sho' wants to go back to my White Pa, but old Bat wouldn't let us go. He come to our quarters dat night and tell mama if she or us chillen try to run off he'll kill us. Dey sho' watch us for awhile.

"Sometimes one of de niggers runs off but he ain't gone long. He gits hongry and comes back. Den he gits a burnin' with de bullwhip. Does he run 'way again, Marse Bat say he got too much rabbit in him and chains him up till he goes to Little Rock and sells him.

"I heared some white folks treat dey slaves good and give dem time off, but Marse Bat don't. We has plenty to eat and clothes, but dat all. Dat de way it was till we's freed, only it wasn't in Arkansas. It was down to Richmond, here in Texas, 'cause Marse Bat rents a farm at Richmond. He thunk if he brung us to Texas he wouldn't have to set us free. But he got fooled, 'cause a gov'ment man come tell us we's free. We had de crop planted and old Bat say if we'll stay through pickin' he'll pay us. Mama and us stayed awhile.

"I gits married legal with Richard Scott and we comes to Harrisburg and he gits a job on de section of de railroad. I's lived here ever since. My husban' and me raises five chillen, but only de one gal am alive now. My grandson takes care of me. He tells me iffen my husband lived so long, he be 107 years old. I know he was older dan me, but not 'xactly how much.

"Sometime I feel I's been here too long, 'cause I's paralyzed and can't move round none. But maybe de

Lawd ain't ready for me yet, and de Debbil won't have me."

ABRAM SELLS

Abram Sells was born a slave on the Rimes Plantation, which was located about 18 miles southeast of Newton, Texas. He does not know his age, but must be well along in the 80's, as his recollections of slavery days are keen. He lives at Jamestown, Texas.

"I was birthed on the Rimes Plantation, now called Harrisburg. My great-grand-daddy's name was Bowser Rimes and he was brung to Texas from Louisiana and die at 138 year old. He's buried on the old Ben Powell place close to Jasper. My grand-daddy, that's John, he lives to be 103 year old and he buried on the Eddy plantation at Jasper. My daddy, Mose Rimes, he die young at 86 and he buried in Jasper County, too. My mammy's name was Phoebe and she was birthed a Rimes nigger and brung to Texas from back in Louisiana. The year slaves was freed I was inherit by a man named Sells, what marry into the Rimes family and that's why my name's Sells, 'cause it change 'long with the marriage. Us was jes' ready to be ship back to Louisiana to the new massa's plantation when the end of the war break up the trip.

"You see, we all had purty good time on Massa Rimes's plantation. None of them carin' 'bout being sot free. They has to work hard all time, but that don' mean so much, 'cause they have to work iffen they was on they own, too. The old folks was 'lowed Saturday evenin' off or when they's sick, and us little ones, us not do much but bring in the wood and kindle the fires and tote water and he'p wash clothes and feed the little pigs and chickens.

"Us chillen hang round close to the big house and us have a old man that went round with us and look after us, white chillen and black chillen, and that old man was my great grand-daddy. Us sho' have to mind him, 'cause iffen we didn't, us sho' have bad luck. He allus have the pocket full of things to conjure with. That rabbit foot, he took it out and he work that on you till you take the creeps and git shakin' all over. Then there's a pocket full of fish scales and he kind of squeak and rattle them in the hand and right then you wish you was dead and promise to do anything. Another thing he allus have in the pocket was a li'l old dry-up turtle, jes' a mud turtle 'bout the size of a man's thumb, the whole thing jes' dry up and dead. With that thing he say he could do mos' anything, but he never use it iffen he ain't have to. A few times I seed him git all tangle up and boddered and he go off by hisself and sot down in a quiet place, take out this very turtle and put it in the palm of the hand and turn it round and round and say somethin' all the time. After while he git everything ontwisted and he come back with a smile on he face and maybe whistlin'.

"They fed all us nigger chillen in a big trough made out'n wood, maybe more a wood tray, dug out'n soft timber like magnolia or cypress. They put it under a tree in the shade in summer time and give each chile a wood spoon, then mix all the food up in the trough and us goes to eatin'. Mos' the food was potlicker, jes' common old potlicker; turnip green and the juice, Irish 'taters and the juice, cabbages and peas and beans, jes' anything what make potlicker. All us git round like so many li'l pigs and then us dish in with our wood spoon till it all gone.

"We has lots of meat at times. Old grand-daddy allus ketchin' rabbit in some kind of trap, mostly make out'n a holler log. He sot 'em round in the garden and sho' kotch the rabbits. And possums, us have a good possum dog, sometimes two or three, and every night you heered them dogs barkin' in the field down by the branch. Sho' 'nuf, they git possum treed and us go git him and parbile him and put him in the oven and bake him plumb tender. Then we stacks sweet 'taters round him and po' the juice over the whole thing. Now, there is somethin' good 'nuf for a king.

"There was lots of deer and turkey and squirrel in the wil' wood and somebody out huntin' nearly every day. Course Massa Rime's folks couldn't eat up all this meat befo' it spile and the niggers allus git a great big part of it. Then we kilt lots of hawgs and then talk 'bout eatin'! O, them chitlin's, sousemeat and the haslets, thats the liver and the lights all biled up together. Us li'l niggers fill up on sich as that and go to bed and mos' dream us is li'l pigs.

"Us allus have plenty to eat but didn't pay much 'tention to clothes. Boys and gals all dress jes' alike, one long shirt or dress. They call it a shirt iffen a boy wear it and call it a dress iffen the gal wear it. There wasn't no difference, 'cause they's all made out'n somethin' like duck and all white. That is, they's white when you fus' put them on, but after you wears them a while they git kind of pig-cullud, kind of grey, but still they's all the same color. Us all go barefoot in summer, li'l ones and big ones, but in winter us have homemake shoes. They tan the leather at home and make the shoe at home, allus some old nigger that kin make shoe. They was more like moc'sin, with lace made of deerskin. The soles was peg on with wood pegs out'n maple and sharpen down with a shoe knife.

"Us have hats make out'n pine straw, long leaf pine straw, tied together in li'l bunches and platted round and round till it make a kinder hat. That pine straw great stuff in them days and us use it in lots of ways. Us kivered sweet 'taters with it to keep them from git freeze and hogs made beds out'n it and folks too. Yes, sir, us slep' on it. The beds had jes' one leg. They bored two hole in the wall up in the corner and stuck two pole in them holes and lay plank on that like slats and pile lots of pine straw on that. Then they spread a homemake blanket or quilt on that and sometime four or five li'l niggers slep' in there to keep us warm.

"The li'l folks slep' mos' as long as they want to in daylight, but the big niggers have to come out'n that bed 'bout fo' o'clock when the big horn blow. The overseer have one nigger, he wake up early for to blow the horn and when he blow this horn he make sich a holler then all the res' of the niggers better git out'n that bed and 'pear at the barn 'bout daylight. He might not whip him for being late the fus' time, but that nigger better not forgit the secon' time and be late!

"Massa Rimes didn't whip them much, but iffen they was bad niggers he jes' sold them offen the place and let somebody else do the whippin'. Never have no church house or school, but Massa Rimes, he call them in and read the Bible to them. Then he turn the service over to some good, old, 'ligious niggers and let them finish with the singin' and prayin' and 'zorting. After peach [HW: "?"] cleared, a school was 'stablish and a white man come from the north to teach the cullud chillen, but befo' that they didn' take no pains to teach the niggers nothin' 'ceptin' to work, and the white chillen didn't have much school neither.

"That was one plantation what was run 'sclusively by itself. Massa Rimes have a commissary or sto' house, whar he kep' whatnot things—them what make on the plantation and things the slaves couldn' make for themselfs. That wasn't much, 'cause we make us own clothes and shoes and plow and all farm tools and us even make our own plow line out'n cotton and iffen us run short of cotton sometime make them out'n bear grass and we make buttons for us clothes out'n li'l round pieces of gourds and kiver them with cloth.

Abram Sells

"That wasn't sich a big plantation, 'bout a t'ousand acre and only 'bout forty niggers. There was'n no jail and they didn't need none. Us have no real doctor, but of course there was a doctor man at Jasper and one at Newton, but a nigger have to be purty sick 'fore they call a doctor. There's allus some old time nigger what knowed lots of remedies and knowed all dif'rent kinds of yarbs and roots. My grand-daddy, he could stop blood, and he could conjure off the fever and rub his fingers over warts and they'd git away. He make ile out'n rattlesnake for the rheumatis'. For the cramp he git a kind of bark offen a tree and it done the job, too. Some niggers wo' brass rings to keep off the rheumatis' and punch hole in a penny or dime and wear that on the ankle to keep off sickness.

"'Member the war? Course I does. I 'member how some of them march off in their uniforms, lookin' so grand, and how some of them hide out in the wood to keep from lookin' so grand. They was lots of talkin' 'bout fighting, and rubbing and scrubbing the old shotgun. The oldes' niggers was settin' round the fire late in the night, stirrin' the ashes with the poker and rakin' out the roas' 'taters. They's smokin' the old corn cob pipe and homemake tobacco and whisperin' right low and quiet like what they's gwineter do and whar they's gwineter to when Mister Lincoln, he turn them free.

"The more they talk, the more I git scared that the niggers is going to git sot free and wondering what I's gwine to do if they is. No, I guess I don't want to live back in them times no mo', but I sho' seed lots of niggers not doin' so well as they did when they was slaves and not havin' nigh as much to eat."

GEORGE SELMAN

George Selman was born in 1852, five miles east of Alto, Texas. His father was born in Virginia and his mother in South Carolina, and were brought to Texas by Mr. Dan Lewis. Green has been a Baptist minister since his youth. He lives in Jacksonville, Texas.

"We was a big fam'ly, nine children. I was born a slave of the Selmans, Marster Tom and Missus Polly, and they lived in Mississippi. Mother's name was Martha and my father's name was John Green Selman.

"Marster's folks come from Mississippi a long ways back and they had a big house made from hewed logs with a big hallway down the middle. The kitchen was out in the yard, 'bout forty steps from the house. The yard had five acres in it and a big garden was in it. Marster had five slave families and our cabins was built in a half circle in the back yard. I seemed to be the pet and always went with Marster Tom to town or wherever he was goin'. Then I learned to plow by my mother letting me hold the handles and walk along with her. Finally she let me go 'round by myself.

"Marster Tom was always good to us and he taught me religion. He was the best man I ever knew. Then Saturday noon come, they blew the horn and we quit workin'. We went to church one Sunday a month and we sat on one side and the white folks on the other.

George Selman

"I never learnt to read and write, but I learned to work in the house and the fields. Late in the day Aunt Dicey, who was the cook, called all us children out under the big trees and give us supper. This was in summer, but nobody ever fed us but Aunt Dicey. We all ate from one bowl, or maybe I'd call it a tray 'cause it was made of wood, like a bread tray but bigger, big enough to hold three, four gallons. She put the food in the tray and give each chil' a spoon. Mostly we had pot likker and corn-bread. In winter we ate from the same tray, but in the kitchen.

"I never seen runaway slaves, but Marster Tom had a neighbor mean to slaves and sometimes when they was whipped we could hear 'em holler. The neighbor had one slave called Sallie, and she was a weaver and was so mean she had to wear a chain. After she died, I heered her ghost one night. I was stayin' with a white man who had the malaria-typhoid-pneumonia fever, and one night I heered Sallie scream and seen her chain drag back and forth. I tol' the man I knowed it was Sallie, 'cause I'd heered that scream for years. But the man said she was dead, so it mus' have been her ghost. I heered her night after night, screamin' and draggin' her chain up and down.

"When Marster Tom says we's free, I goes to his sister, Miss Ca'line and works for her. After sev'ral years I larned to preach and I's the author of most the Baptist churches in this county."

CALLIE SHEPHERD

Callie Shepherd, age 84, lives at 4701 Spring Ave., Dallas, Texas. She was born near Gilmer, Texas, in 1852, a slave of the Stevens family. At present she is cared for by her 68 year old son and his wife.

"Course I kin tell you. I got 'memberance like dey don't have nowadays. Dat 'cause things is goin' round and round too fast without no settin' and talkin' things over.

"I's native born right down here at Gilmer on de old place and Miss Fannie could tell you de same if she could be in your presence, but she went on to Glory many a year ago. She de one what raised me, right in de house with her own chillen. I slep' right in de house, in de chillens' room, in a little trundle bed what jus' pushed back under de big bed when de mornin' come. If her chillen et one side de table I et t'other side, right by Miss Fannie's elbow.

"Miss Fannie, she Dr. Steven's wife and dey from Georgia and lived near Gilmer till de doctor goes off to de war and takes a sickness what he ain't never get peart from and died. Died right there on de old place. He was a right livin' man and dey allus good to me and my mammy, what dey done brought from Georgia and she de main cook.

"My mammy don't think they ain't nobody like Miss Fannie. My mammy, she a little red-Indian nigger woman not so big as me, and Miss Fanny tell her, 'Don't you cry 'cause dey tryin' make freedom, 'cause de doctor done say we is gwine help you raise your babies.'

"Some de niggers don't like de treatment what dey white folks gives 'em and dey run away to de woods. I'd hear de nigger dogs a-runnin' and when dey cotch de niggers dey bites 'em all over and tears dey clothes and gits de skin, too. And de niggers, dey'd holler. I seed 'em whip de niggers, 'cause dey tolt de chillen to look. Dey buckled 'em down on de groun' and laid it on dey backs. Sometimes dey laid on with a mighty heavy hand. But I ain't never git no whippin' 'cause I never went with de cullud gen'ration. I set right in de buggy with de white chillen and went to hear Gospel preachin'.

Callie Shepherd

"I danced at de balls in de sixteen figure round sets and everybody in dem parts say I de principal dancer, but I gits 'ligion and left de old way to live in de 'termination to live beyon' dis vale of tears.

"I have my trib'lations after my old daddy die, 'cause

he good to us little chillen. But my next daddy a man mighty rough on us. Dat after Miss Fannie done gone back to Georgia and my back done hurt me all de time from pullin' fodder and choppin' cotton. It make a big indif'rence after Miss Fannie gone, and de war de cause of it all. I heered de big cannons goin' on over there jus' like de bigges' clap of thunder.

"Me and de little chillen playin' in de road makin' frog houses out of sand when we hear de hosses comin'. We looks and see de budallions shinin' in de sun and de sojers have tin cups tied on side dere saddles and throwed dem cups to us chillen as dey passed. Dey say war is over and we is free. Miss Fannie say she a Seay from Georgia and she go back dere, but I jus' stay on where I's native born."

BETTY SIMMONS

Betty Simmons, 100 or more, was born a slave to Leftwidge Carter, in Macedonia, Alabama. She was stolen when a child, sold to slave traders and later to a man in Texas. She now lives in Beaumont, Texas.

"I think I's 'bout a hunnerd and one or two year old. My papa was a free man, 'cause his old massa sot him free 'fore I's born, and give him a hoss and saddle and a little house to live in.

"My old massa when I's a chile, he name Mr. Leftwidge Carter and when he daughter marry Mr. Wash Langford, massa give me to her. She was call Clementine. Massa Langford has a little store and a man call Mobley go in business with him. Dis man brung down he two brothers and dey fair clean Massa Langford out. He was ruint.

"But while all dis goin' on I didn't know it and I was happy. Dey was good to me and I don't work too hard, jus' gits in de mischief. One time I sho' got drunk and dis de way of it. Massa have de puncheon of whiskey and he sell de whiskey, too. Now, in dem days, dey have frills 'round de beds, dey wasn't naked beds like nowdays. Dey puts dis puncheon under de beds and de frills hides it, but I's nussin' a little boy in dat room and I crawls under dat bed and drinks out of de puncheon. Den I poke de head out and say 'Boo' at de little boy, and he laugh and laugh. Den I ducks back and drinks a little more and I say 'Boo' at him 'gain, and he laugh and laugh. Dey was lots of whiskey in dat puncheon and I keeps drinkin' and sayin' 'Boo'. My head, it gits funny and I come out with de puncheon and starts to de kitchen, where my aunt Adeline was de cook. I jes' a-stompin' and sayin' de big words. Dey never lets me 'round where dat puncheon is no more.

"When Massa Langford was ruint and dey goin' take de store 'way from him, dey was trouble, plenty of dat. One day massa send me down to he brudder's place. I was dere two days and den de missy tell me to go to de fence. Dere was two white men in a buggy and one of 'em say, 'I thought she bigger dan dat.' Den he asks me, 'Betty, kin you cook?' I tells him I been cook helper two, three month, and he say, 'You git dressed and came on down three mile to de other side de post office.' So I gits my little bundle and whan I gits dere he say, 'Gal, you want to go 'bout 26 mile and help cook at de boardin' house?' He tries to make me believe I won't be gone a long time, but when I gits in de buggy dey tells me Massa Langford done los' everything and he have to hide out he niggers for to keep he credickers from gittin' dem. Some of de niggers he hides in de woods, but he stole me from my sweet missy and sell me so dem credickers can't git me.

"When we gits to de crossroads dere de massa and a nigger man. Dat another slave he gwine to sell, and he hate to sell us so bad he can't look us in de eye. Dey puts us niggers inside de buggy, so iffen de credickers comes along dey can't see us.

"Finally dese slave spec'laters puts de nigger man and me on de train and takes us to Memphis, and when we gits dere day takes us to de nigger traders' yard. We gits dere at breakfast time and waits for de boat dey calls de 'Ohio' to git dere. De boat jus' ahead of dis Ohio, Old Capt. Fabra's boat, was 'stroyed and dat delay our boat two hours. When it come, dey was 258 niggers out of dem nigger yards in Memphis what gits on dat boat. Dey puts de niggers upstairs and goes down de river far as Vicksburg, dat was de place, and den us gits offen de boat and gits on de train 'gain and dat time we goes to New Orleans.

"I's satisfy den I los' my people and ain't never goin' to see dem no more in dis world, and I never did. Dey has three big trader yard in New Orleans and I hear de traders say dat town 25 mile square. I ain't like it so well, 'cause I ain't like it 'bout dat big river. We hears some of 'em say dere's gwineter throw a long war and us all think what dey buy us for if we's gwine to be sot free. Some was still buyin' niggers every fall and us think it too funny dey kep' on fillin' up when dey gwineter be emptyin' out soon.

"Dey have big sandbars and planks fix 'round de nigger yards and dey have watchmans to keep dem from runnin 'way in de swamp. Some of de niggers dey have jus' picked up on de road, dey steals dem. Dey calls dem 'wagon boy' and 'wagon gal.' Dey has one bit mulatto boy dey stole 'long de road dat way and he massa find out 'bout him and come and git him and take him 'way. And a woman what was a seamster, a man what knowed her seed her in de pen and he done told her massa and he come right down and git her. She sho' was proud to git out. She was stole from 'long de road, too. You sees, if dey could steal de niggers and sell 'em for de good money, dem traders could make plenty money dat way.

"At las' Col. Fortescue, he buy me and kep' me. He a fighter in de Mexican war and he come to New Orleans to buy he slaves. He takes me up de Red River to Shreveport and den by de buggy to Liberty, in Texas.

"De Colonel, he a good massa to us. He 'lows us to work de patch of ground for ourselves, and maybe have a pig or a couple chickens for ourselves, and he allus make out to give us plenty to eat.

"De massa, when a place fill up, he allus pick and move to a place where dere ain't so much people. Dat how come de Colonel fus' left Alabama and come to Texas, and to de place dey calls Beef Head den, but calls Gran' Cane now.

"When us come to Gran' Cane a nigger boy git stuck on one us house girls and he run away from he massa and foller us. It were a woodly country and de boy outrun he chasers. I heered de dogs after him and he torn and bleedin' with de bresh and he run upstair in de gin house. De dogs sot down by de door and de dog-man, what hired to chase him, he drug him down and throw him in de Horse Hole and tells de two dogs to swim in and git him. De boy so scairt he yell and holler but de dogs nip and pinch him good with de claws and teeth. When dey lets de boy out de water hole he all bit up and when he massa larn how mean de dog-man been to de boy he 'fuses to pay de fee.

"I gits married in slavery time, to George Fortescue. De massa he marry us sort of like de justice of de peace. But my husban', he git kilt in Liberty, when he cuttin' down a tree and it fall on him. I ain't never marry no more.

"I sho' was glad when freedom come, 'cause dey jus' ready to put my little three year old boy in de field. Dey took 'em young. I has another baby call Mittie, and she too young to work. I don't know how many chillen I's have, and sometimes I sits and tries to count 'em. Dey's seven livin' but I had 'bout fourteen.

Betty Simmons

"Dey was pretty hard on de niggers. Iffen us have de baby us only 'lowed to stay in de house for one month and card and spin, and den us has to get out in de field.

Dey allus blow de horn for us mammies to come up and nuss de babies.

"I seed plenty soldiers 'fore freedom. Dey's de Democrats, 'cause I never seed no Yankees. Us niggers used to wash and iron for dem. At night us seed dose soldiers peepin' 'round de house and us run 'way in de bresh.

"When freedom come us was layin' by de crop and de massa he give us a gen'rous part of dat crop and us move to Clarks place. We gits on all right after freedom, but it hard at first 'cause us didn't know how to do for ourselves. But we has to larn."

GEORGE SIMMONS

George Simmons, born in Alabama in 1854, was owned by Mr. Steve Jaynes, who lived near Beaumont, Texas. George has a good many memories of slavery years, although he was still a child when he was freed. He now lives in Beaumont, Tex.

"I's bo'n durin' slavery, somewhar in Alabama, but I don' 'member whar my mammy said. Dey brung me here endurin' de War and I belonged to Massa Steve Jaynes, and he had 'bout 75 other niggers. It was a big place and lots of wo'k, but I's too little to do much 'cept errands 'round de house.

"Massa Jaynes, he raised cotton and co'n and he have 'bout 400 acres. He 'spected de niggers to wo'k hard from mornin' till sundown, but he was fair in treatin' 'em. He give us plenty to eat and lots of cornbread and black-eye' peas and plenty hawg meat and sich. We had possum sometimes, too. Jus' took a nice, fat possum we done cotched in de woods and skinned 'im and put 'im in a oven and roas' 'im with sweet 'tatoes all 'round and make plenty gravy. Dat was good.

"Massa Jaynes, he 'lowed de slaves who wanted to have a little place to make garden, veg'tables and dose kin' of things. He give 'em seed and de nigger could have all he raised in his little garden. We was all well kep' and

I don' see whar freedom was much mo' better, in a way. Course, some massas was bad to dere slaves and whipped 'em so ha'd dey's nearly dead. I know dat, 'cause I heered it from de neighbors places. Some of dere slaves would run away and hide in de woods and mos' of 'em was kotched with dogs. Fin'ly dey took to puttin' bells on de slaves so iffen dey run away, dey could hear 'em in de woods. Dey put 'em on with a chain, so dey couldn' get 'em off.

"We could have church on Sunday and our own cullud church. Sam Watson, he was de nigger preacher and he's a slave, too.

George Simmons

"I didn' know much 'bout de war, 'cause we couldn' read and de white folks didn' talk war much 'fore us. But we heered things and I 'member de sojers on dere way back after it's all over. Dey wasn' dressed in a uniform and dey clothes was mos'ly rags, dey was dat tore up. We seed 'em walkin' on de road and sometimes dey had ole wagons, but mos' times dey walk. I 'member some Yankee sojers, too. Dey have canteens over de shoulder, and mos' of 'em has blue uniforms on.

"Massa, he tell us when freedom come, and some of us stays 'round awhile, 'cause whar is we'uns goin'? We didn' know what to do and we didn' know how to keep ourselves, and what was we to do to get food and a place to live? Dose was ha'd times, 'cause de country tore up and de business bad.

"And de Kluxes dey range 'round some. Dey soon plays out but dey took mos' de time to scare de niggers. One time dey comes to my daddy's house and de leader, him in de long robe, he say, 'Nigger, quick you and git me a drink of water.' My daddy, he brung de white folks drinkin' gourd and dat Klux, he say, 'Nigger, I say git me a big drink—bring me dat bucket. I's thirsty.' He drinks three buckets of water, we thinks he does, but what you think we learns? He has a rubber bag under his robe and is puttin' dat water in dere!"

BEN SIMPSON

Ben Simpson, 90, was born in Norcross, Georgia, a slave of the Stielszen family. He had a cruel master, and was afraid to tell the truth about his life as a slave, until assured that no harm would come to him. Ben now lives in Madisonville, Texas, and receives a small old age pension.

"Boss, I's born in Georgia, in Norcross, and I's ninety years old. My father's name was Roger Stielszen and my mother's name was Betty. Massa Earl Stielszen captures them in Africa and brung them to Georgia. He got kilt and my sister and me went to his son. His son was a killer. He got in trouble there in Georgia and got him two good-stepping hosses and the covered wagon. Then he chains all he slaves round the necks and fastens the chains to the hosses and makes then walk all the way to Texas. My mother and my sister had to walk. Emma was my sister. Somewhere on the road it went to snowin' and massa wouldn't let us wrap anything round our feet. We had to sleep on the ground, too, in all that snow.

"Massa have a great, long whip platted out of rawhide and when one the niggers fall behind or give out, he hit him with that whip. It take the hide every time he hit a nigger. Mother, she give out on the way, 'bout the line of Texas. Her feet got raw and bleedin' and her legs swoll plumb out of shape. Then massa, he jus' take out he gun and shot her, and whilst she lay dyin' he kicks her two, three times and say, 'Damn a nigger what can't stand nothin'.' Boss, you know that man, he wouldn't bury mother, jus' leave her layin' where he shot her at. You know, then there wasn't no law 'gainst killin' nigger slaves.

"He come plumb to Austin through that snow. He taken up farmin' and changes he name to Alex Simpson, and changes our names, too. He cut logs and builded he home on the side of them mountains. We never had no quarters. When night-time come he locks the chain round our necks and then locks it round a tree. Boss, our bed were the ground. All he feed us was raw meat and green corn. Boss, I et many a green weed. I was hongry. He never let us eat at noon, he worked us all day without stoppin'. We went naked, that the way he worked us. We never had any clothes.

"He brands us. He brand my mother befo' us left Georgia. Boss, that nearly kilt her. He brand her in the breast, then between the shoulders. He brand all us.

"My sister, Emma, was the only woman he have till he marries. Emma was wife of all seven Negro slaves. He sold her when she's 'bout fifteen, jus' befo' her baby was born. I never seen her since.

"Boss, massa was a outlaw. He come to Texas and deal in stolen hosses. Jus' befo' he's hung for stealin' hosses, he marries a young Spanish gal. He sho' mean to her. Whips her 'cause she want him to leave he slaves alone and live right. Bless her heart, she's the best gal in the world. She was the best thing God ever put life in the world. She cry and cry every time massa go off. She let us a-loose and she feed us good one time while he's gone. Missy Selena, she turn us a-loose and we wash in the creek clost by. She jus' fasten the chain on us and give us great big pot cooked meat and corn, and up he rides. Never says a word but come to see what us eatin'. He pick up he whip and whip her till she falls. If I could have got a-loose I'd kilt him. I swore if I ever got a-loose I'd kill him. But befo' long after that he fails to come home, and some people finds him hangin' to a tree. Boss, that long after war time he got hung. He didn't let us free. We wore chains all the time. When we work, we drug them chains with us. At night he lock us to a tree to keep us from runnin' off. He didn't have to do that. We were 'fraid to run. We knew he'd kill us. Besides, he brands us and they no way to get it off. It's put there with a hot iron. You can't git it off.

"If a slave die, massa made the rest of us tie a rope round he feet and drug him off. Never buried one, it was too much trouble.

"Massa allus say he be rich after the war. He stealin' all the time. He have a whole mountain side where he keep he stock. Missy Selena tell us one day we sposed to be free, but he didn't turn us a-loose. It was 'bout three years after the war they hung him. Missy turned us a-loose.

"I had a hard time then. All I had to eat was what I could find and steal. I was 'fraid of everybody. I jus' went wild and to the woods, but, thank God, a bunch of men taken they dogs and run me down. They carry me to they place. Gen. Houston had some niggers and he made them feed me. He made them keep me till I git well and able to work. Then he give me a job. I marry one the gals befo'

I leaves them. I'm plumb out of place there at my own weddin'. Yes, suh, boss, it wasn't one year befo' that I'm the wild nigger. We had thirteen chillen.

"I farms all my life after that. I didn't know nothin' else to do. I made plenty cotton, but now I'm too old. Me and my wife is alone now. This old nigger gits the li'l pension from the gov'ment. I not got much longer to stay here. I's ready to see God but I hope my old massa ain't there to torment me again."

GILES SMITH

Giles Smith, 79, now residing at 3107 Blanchard St., Fort Worth, Texas, was born a slave of Major Hardway, on a plantation near Union Springs, Alabama. The Major gave Giles to his daughter when he was an infant and he never saw his parents again. In 1874 Frank Talbot brought Giles to Texas, and he worked on the farm two years. He then went to Brownwood and worked in a gin seventeen years. In 1908 he moved to Fort Worth and worked for a packing company. Old age led to his discharge in 1931 and he has since worked at any odd jobs he could find.

"My name am Giles Smith, 'cause my pappy was born on the Smith plantation and I took his name. I's born at Union Springs, in Alabama and Major Hardway owned me and 'bout a hundred other slaves. But he gave me to Mary, his daughter, when I's only a few months old and had to be fed on a bottle, 'cause she am jus' married to Massa Miles. She told me how she carried me home in her arms. She say I was so li'l she have a hard time to make me eat out the bottle, and I put up a good fight so she nearly took me back.

"I don't 'member the start of the war, but de endin' I does. Massa Miles called all us together and told us we's free and it give us all de jitters. He treated all us fine and nobody wanted to go. He and Missy am de best folks de Lawd could make. I stayed till I was sixteen years old.

"It am years after freedom Missy Mary say to me what massa allus say, 'If the nigger won't follow orders by kind treatin', sich nigger am wrong in the head and not worth keepin'. He didn't have to rush us. We'd just dig in and do the work. One time Massa clearin' some land and it am gittin' late for breakin' the ground. Us allus have Saturday afternoon and Sunday off. Old Jerry says to us, 'Tell yous what us do,—go to the clearin' this afternoon and Sunday and finish for the Massa. That sho' make him glad.'

"Saturday noon came and nobody tells the massa but go to that clearin' and sing while us work, cuttin' bresh and grubbin' stomps and burnin' bresh. Us sing

> "'Hi, ho, ug, hi, ho, ug.
> De sharp bit, de strong arm,
> Hi, ho, ug, hi, ho, ug,
> Dis tree am done 'fore us warm.'

"De massa come out and his mouth am slippin' all over he face and he say, 'What this all mean? Why you workin' Saturday afternoon?'

"Old Jerry am a funny cuss and he say, 'Massa, O, massa, please don't whop us for cuttin' down yous trees.'

"'I's gwine whop you with the chicken stew,' Massa say. And for Sunday dinner dere am chicken stew with noodles and peach cobbler.

"So I stays with massa and after I's fifteen he pays me $2.00 the month, and course I gits my eats and my clothes, too. When I gits the first two I don't know what to do, 'cause it the first money I ever had. Missy make the propulation to keep the money and buy for me and teach me 'bout it. There ain't much to buy, 'cause we make nearly everything right there. Even the tobaccy am made. They put honey 'twixt the leaves and put a pile of it 'twixt two boards with weights. It am left for a month and that am a man's tobaccy. A weaklin' better stay off that kind tobaccy.

"First I works in the field and then am massa's coachman. But when I's 'bout sixteen I gits a idea to go off somewheres for myself. I hears 'bout Mr. Frank Talbot, whom am takin' some niggers to Texas and I goes with him to the Brazos River bottom, and works there two years. I's lonesome for massa and missy and if I'd been clost enough, I'd sho' gone back to the old plantation. So after two years I quits and goes to work for Mr. Winfield Scott down in Brownwood, in the gin, for seventeen years.

"Well, shortly after I gits to Brownwood I meets a yaller gal and after dat I don't care to go back to Alabama so hard. I's married to Dee Smith on December the eighteenth, in 1880, and us live together many years. She died six years ago. Us have six chillen but I don't know where one of them are now. They all forgit their father in his old age! They not so young, either.

Giles Smith

"My woman could write a little so she write missy for me, and she write back and wish us luck and if we ever wants to come back to the old home we is welcome. Us write back' forth with her. Finally, us git the letter what say she sick, and then awful low. That 'bout twenty-five years after I marries. That am too much for me, and I catches the next train back to Alabama but I gits there too late. She am dead, and I never has forgive myself, 'cause I don't go back befo' she die, like she ask us to, lots of times.

"I comes here fifteen years ago and here I be. The last six year I can't work in the packin' plants no more. I's too old. Anything I can find to do I does, but it ain't much no more.

"The worst grief I's had, am to think I didn't go see missy 'fore she die. I's never forgave myself for that."

United States. Work Projects Administration

JAMES W. SMITH

James W. Smith, 77, was born a slave of the Hallman family, in Palestine, Texas. James became a Baptist minister in 1895, and preached until 1931, when poor health forced him to retire. He and his wife live at 1306 E. Fourth St., Fort Worth, Texas.

"Yes, suh, I'm birthed a slave, but never worked as sich, 'cause I's too young. But I 'members hearin' my mother tell all about her slave days and our master. He was John Hallman and owned a place in Palestine, with my mother and father and fifty other slaves. My folks was house servants and lived a little better'n the field hands. De cabins was built cheap, though, no money, only time for buildin' am de cost. Dey didn't use nails and helt de logs in place by dovetailin'. Dey closed de space between de logs with wedges covered with mud and straw. De framework for de door was helt by wooden pegs and so am de benches and tables. Master Hallman always had some niggers trained for carpenter work, and one to be blacksmith and one to make shoes and harness.

"We was lucky to have de kind master, what give us plenty to eat. If all de people now could have jus' so good food what we had, there wouldn't be no beggin' by hungry folks or need for milk funds for starved babies.

"We didn't have purty clothes sich as now, with all de

dif'rent colors mixed up, but dey was warm and lastin', dyed brown and black. De black oak and cherry made de dyes. Our shoes wasn't purty, either. I has to laugh when I think of de shoes. There wasn't no careful work put on dem, but dey covered de feets and lasted near forever.

"Master always wanted to help his cullud folks live right and my folks always said de best time of they lives was on de old plantation. He always 'ranged for parties and sich. Yes, suh, he wanted dem to have a good time, but no foolishment, jus' good, clean fun. There am dancin' and singin' mostest every Saturday night. He had a little platform built for de jiggin' contests. Cullud folks comes from all round, to see who could jig de best. Sometimes two niggers each put a cup of water on de head and see who could jig de hardest without spillin' any. It was lots of fun.

"I must tell you 'bout de best contest we ever had. One nigger on our place was de jigginest fellow ever was. Everyone round tries to git somebody to best him. He could put de glass of water on his head and make his feet go like triphammers and sound like de snaredrum. He could whirl round and sich, all de movement from his hips down. Now it gits noised round a fellow been found to beat Tom and a contest am 'ranged for Saturday evenin'. There was a big crowd and money am bet, but master bets on Tom, of course.

"So dey starts jiggin'. Tom starts easy and a little faster and faster. The other fellow doin' de same. Dey gits faster and faster and dat crowd am a-yellin'. Gosh! There am 'citement. Dey jus' keep a-gwine. It look like Tom done found his match, but there am one thing yet he ain't done—he ain't made de whirl. Now he does it.

Everyone holds he breath, and de other fellow starts to make de whirl and he makes it, but jus' a spoonful of water sloughs out his cup, so Tom am de winner.

"When freedom come, the master tells his slaves and says, 'What you gwine do?' Wall, suh, not one of dem knows dat. De fact am, dey's scared dey gwine be put off de place. But master says dey can stay and work for money or share crop. He says they might be trouble 'twixt de whites and niggers and likely it be best to stay and not git mixed in dis and dat org'ization. Mostest stays, only one or two goes away. My folks stays for five years after de war. Den my father moves to Bertha Creek, where he done 'range for a farm of his own. They hated to leave master's plantation, he's so good and kind.

"Some the cullud folks thinks they's to take charge and run the gov'ment. They asks my father to jine their org'ization. He goes once and some eggs am served. Dey am served by de crowd and dem eggs ain't fresh yard eggs. Father 'cides he wants his eggs served dif'rent, and he likes dem fresh, so he takes master's advice and don't jine nothing.

"When de Klux come, de cullud org'ization made their scatterment. Plenty gits whipped round our place and some what wasn't 'titled to it. Den soldiers comes and puts order in de section. Dey has trouble about votin'. De cullud folks in dem days was non-knowledge, so how could dey vote 'telligent? Dat am foolishment to 'sist on de right to vote. It de non-knowledge what hurts. Myself, I never voted and am too far down de road now to start.

James W. Smith

"I worked at farmin' till 1895 when I starts preachin' in de Baptist church. I kept that up till 1931, but my health got too bad and I had to quit. I has de pressure bad. When

I preaches, I preaches hard, and de doctor says dat am danger for me.

"The way I learns to preach am dis: after surrender, I 'tends de school two terms and den I studies de Bible and I's a nat'ral talker and gifted for de Lawd's work, so I starts preachin'.

"Jennie Goodman and me marries in 1885 and de Lawd never blessed us with any chillen. We gits de pension, me $16.00 and her $14.00, and gits by on dat. It am for de rations and de eats, but de clothes am a question!"

United States. Work Projects Administration

JORDON SMITH

Jordon Smith, 86, was born in Georgia, a slave of the Widow Hicks. When she died, Jordon, his mother and thirty other slaves were willed to Ab Smith, his owner's nephew, and were later refugeed from Georgia to Anderson Co., Texas. When freed, Jordon worked on a steamboat crew on the Red River until the advent of railroads. For thirty years Jordon worked for the railroad. He is now too feeble to work and lives with his third wife and six children in Marshall, Texas, supported by the latter and his pension of $10.00 a month.

"I's borned in Georgia, next to the line of North Car'lina, on Widow Hick's place. My papa died 'fore I's borned but my mammy was called Aggie. My ole missus died and us fell to her nephew, Ab Smith. My granma and granpa was full-blooded Africans and I couldn't unnerstand their talk.

"My missus was borned on the Chattahoochee River and she had 2,000 acres of land in cul'vation, a thousand on each side the river, and owned 500 slaves and 250 head of work mules. She was the richest woman in the whole county.

"Us slaves lived in a double row log cabins facin' her house and our beds was made of rough plank and mattresses of hay and lynn bark and shucks, make on a machine. I's spinned many a piece of cloth and wove many a brooch of thread.

"Missus didn't 'low her niggers to work till they's 21, and the chillen played marbles and run round and kick their heels. The first work I done was hoeing and us worked long as we could see a stalk of cotton or hill of corn. Missus used to call us at Christmas and give the old folks a dollar and the rest a dinner. When she died me and my mother went to Ab Smith at the dividement of the property. Master Ab put us to work on a big farm he bought and it was Hell 'mong the yearlin's if you crost him or missus either. It was double trouble and a cowhidin' whatever you do. She had a place in the kitchen where she tied their hands up to the wall and cowhided them and sometimes cut they back 'most to pieces. She made all go to church and let the women wear some her old, fine dresses to hide the stripes where she'd beat them. Mammy say that to keep the folks at church from knowin' how mean she was to her niggers.

"Master Ab had a driver and if you didn't do what that driver say, master say to him, 'Boy, come here and take this nigger down, a hunerd licks this time.' Sometimes us run off and go to a dance without a pass and 'bout time they's kickin' they heels and getting sot for the big time, in come a patterroller and say, 'Havin' a big time, ain't you? Got a pass?' If you didn't, they'd git four or five men to take you out and when they got through you'd sho' go home.

"Master Ab had hunerds acres wheat and made the women stack hay in the field. Sometimes they got sick and wanted to go to the house, but he made them lay down on a straw-pile in the field. Lots of chillen was borned on a straw-pile in the field. After the chile was borned he sent them to the house. I seed that with my own eyes.

"They was a trader yard in Virginia and one in New Orleans and sometimes a thousand slaves was waitin' to be sold. When the traders knowed men was comin' to buy, they made the slaves all clean up and greased they mouths with meat skins to look like they's feedin' them plenty meat. They lined the women up on one side and the men on the other. A buyer would walk up and down 'tween the two rows and grab a woman and try to throw her down and feel of her to see how she's put up. If she's purty strong, he'd say, 'Is she a good breeder?' If a gal was 18 or 19 and put up good she was worth 'bout $1,500. Then the buyer'd pick out a strong, young nigger boy 'bout the same age and buy him. When he got them home he'd say to them, 'I want you two to stay together. I want young niggers.'

"If a nigger ever run off the place and come back, master'd say, 'If you'll be a good nigger, I'll not whip you this time.' But you couldn't 'lieve that. A nigger run off and stayed in the woods six month. When he come back he's hairy as a cow, 'cause he lived in a cave and come out at night and pilfer round. They put the dogs on him but couldn't cotch him. Fin'ly he come home and master say he won't whip him and Tom was crazy 'nough to 'lieve it. Master say to the cook, 'Fix Tom a big dinner,' and while Tom's eatin', master stand in the door with a whip and say, 'Tom, I's change my mind; you have no business runnin' off and I's gwine take you out jus' like you come into the world.

"Master gits a bottle whiskey and a box cigars and have Tom tied up out in the yard. He takes a chair and say to the driver, 'Boy, take him down, 250 licks this time.' Then he'd count the licks. When they's 150 licks it didn't look like they is any place left to hit, but master say, 'Finish him up.' Then he and the driver sot down, smoke cigars and drink whiskey, and master tell Tom how he must mind he master. Then he lock Tom up in a log house and master tell all the niggers if they give him anything to eat he'll skin 'em alive. The old folks slips Tom bread and meat. When he gits out, he's gone to the woods 'gain. They's plenty niggers what stayed in the woods till surrender.

"I heared some slaves say they white folks was good to 'em, but it was a tight fight where us was. I's thought over the case a thousand times and figured it was 'cause all men ain't made alike. Some are bad and some are good. It's like that now. Some folks you works for got no heart and some treat you white. I guess it allus will be that way.

"They was more ghosts and hants them days than now. It look like when I's comin' up they was common as pig tracks. They come in different forms and shapes, sometimes like a dog or cat or goat or like a man. I didn't 'lieve in 'em till I seed one. A fellow I knowed could see 'em every time he went out. One time us walkin' 'long a country lane and he say, 'Jordon, look over my right shoulder.' I looked and see a man walkin' without a head. I broke and run plumb off from the man I's with. He wasn't scart of 'em.

"I's refugeed from Georgia to Anderson County 'fore the war. I see Abe Lincoln onct when he come through, but didn't none of know who he was. I heared the president wanted 'em to work the young niggers till they was twenty-one but to free the growed slaves. They say he give 'em thirty days to 'siderate it. The white folks said they'd wade blood saddle deep 'fore they'd let us loose. I don't blame 'em in a way, 'cause they paid for us. In 'nother way it was right to free us. We was brought here and no person is sposed to be made a brute.

Jordon Smith

"After surrender, Massa Ab call us and say we could go. Mammy stayed but I left with my uncles and aunts and went to Shreveport where the Yanks was. I didn't hear from my mammy for the nex' twenty years.

"In Ku Klux times they come to our house and I stood tremblin', but they didn't bother us. I heared 'em say lots of niggers was took down in Sabine bottom and Kluxed, just 'cause they wanted to git rid of 'em. I think it was desperados what done that, 'stead of the Ku Klux. That was did in Panola County, in the Bad Lands. Bill Bateman and Hulon Gresham and Sidney Farney was desperados and would kill a nigger jus' to git rid of him. Course, lots of folks was riled up at the Kluxers and blamed 'em for everything.

"I's voted here in Marshall. Every nation has a flag but the cullud race. The flag is what protects 'em. We wasn't invited here, but was brought here, and don't have no place else to go. We was brought under this government and it's right we be led and told what to do. The cullud folks has been here more'n a hunerd years and has help make the United States what it is. The only thing that'll help the cause is separation of the races. I'll not be here when it comes, but it's bound to, 'cause the Bible say that some day all the races of people will be separated. Since 1865 till now the cullud race have done nothing but go to destruction. There was a time a man could control his wife and family, but you can't do that now.

"After surrender I went to Shreveport and steamboated from there to New Orleans, then to Vicksburg. Old hands was paid $15.00 a trip. I come here in 1872 and railroaded 30 years, on the section gang and in the shops. Since then I farmed and I's had three wives and nineteen chillen and they are scattered all over the state. Since I's too old to farm I work at odd jobs and git a $10.00 a month pension."

United States. Work Projects Administration

MILLIE ANN SMITH

Millie Ann Smith was born in 1850, in Rusk Co., Texas, a slave of George Washington Trammell, a pioneer planter of the county. Trammell bought Millie's mother and three older children in Mississippi before Millie's birth, and brought them to Texas, leaving Millie's father behind. Later he ran away to Texas and persuaded Trammell to buy him, so he could be with his family.

"I's born 'fore war started and 'members when it ceased. I guess mammy's folks allus belonged to the Trammells, 'cause I 'member my grandpa, Josh Chiles, and my grandma, call Jeanette. I's a strappin' big girl when they dies. Grandpa used to say he come to Texas with Massa George Trammell's father when Rusk County was jus' a big woods, and the first two years he was hunter for the massa. He stay in the woods all the time, killing deer and wild hawgs and turkeys and coons and the like for the white folks to eat, and the land's full of Indians. He kinda taken up with them and had holes in the nose and ears. They was put there by the Indians for rings what they wore. Grandpa could talk mos' any Indian talk and he say he used to run off from his massa and stay with the Indians for weeks. The massa'd go to the Indian camp looking for grandpa and the Indians hided him out and say, 'No see him.'

"How mammy and we'uns come to Texas, Massa George brung his wife and three chillen from Mississippi and he brung we'uns. Pappy belonged to Massa Moore over in Mississippi and Massa George didn't buy him, but after mammy got here, that 'fore I's born, pappy runs off and makes his way to Texas and gits Massa George to buy him.

"Massa George and Missy America lived in a fine, big house and they owned more slaves and land than anybody in the county and they's the richest folks 'round there. Us slaves lived down the hill from the big house in a double row of log cabins and us had good beds, like our white folks. My grandpa made all the beds for the white folks and us niggers, too. Massa didn't want anything shoddy 'round him, he say, not even his nigger quarters.

"I's sot all day handin' thread to my mammy to put in the loom, 'cause they give us homespun clothes, and you'd better keep 'em if you didn't want to go naked.

"Massa had a overseer and nigger driver call Jacob Green. If a nigger was hard to make do the right thing, they ties him to a tree, but Massa George never whip 'em too hard, jus' 'nough to make 'em 'have.

"The slaves what worked in the fields was woke up 'fore light with a horn and worked till dark, and then there was the stock to tend to and cloth to weave. The overseer come 'round at nine o'clock to see if all is in the bed and then go back to his own house. When us knowed he's sound asleep we'd slip out and run 'round, sometimes. They locked the young men up in a house at night and on Sunday to keep 'em from runnin' 'round. It was a log house and had cracks in it and once a little nigger boy pokes his hand in tryin' to tease them men and one of 'em chops his fingers off with the ax.

"Massa didn' 'low no nigger to read and write, if he knowed it. George Wood was the only one could read and write and how he larn, a little boy on the 'jining place took up with him and they goes off in the woods and he shows George how to read and write. Massa never did find out 'bout that till after freedom.

"We slips off and have prayer but daren't 'low the white folks know it and sometime we hums 'ligious songs low like when we's workin'. It was our way of prayin' to be free, but the white folks didn't know it. I 'member mammy used to sing like this:

> "'Am I born to die, to lay this body down.
> Must my tremblin' spirit fly into worlds unknown,
> The land of deepes' shade,
> Only pierce' by human thought.'

"Massa George 'lowed them what wanted to work a little ground for theyselves and grandpa made money sellin' wild turkey and hawgs to the poor white folks. He used to go huntin' at night or jus' when he could.

Millie Ann Smith

"Them days we made our own med'cine out of horsemint and butterfly weed and Jerusalem oak and bottled them teas up for the winter. Butterfly Weed tea was for the pleurisy and the others for the chills and fever. As reg'lar as I got up I allus drank my asafoetida and tar water.

"I 'member Massa George furnishes three of his niggers, Ed Chile and Jacob Green and Job Jester, for mule skinners. I seed the government come and take off a big bunch of mules off our place. Mos' onto four year after the war, three men comes to Massa George and makes him call us up and turn us loose. I heered 'em say its close onto four year we's been free, but that's the first we knowed 'bout it.

"Pappy goes to work at odd jobs and mammy and I goes to keep house for a widow woman and I stays there till I marries, and that to Tom Smith. We had five chillen and now Tom's dead and I lives on that pension from the government, what is $16.00 a month, and I's glad to git it, 'cause I's too old to work."

United States. Work Projects Administration

SUSAN SMITH

Susan Smith is not sure of her age, but appears to be in the late eighties. She was a slave of Charles Weeks, in Iberia, Louisiana. Susan was dressed in a black and white print, a light blue apron and a black velvet hat when interviewed, and seemed to be enjoying the generous quid of tobacco she took as she started to tell her story.

"I 'lieve I was nine or ten when freedom come, 'cause I was nursing for the white folks. Old massa was Charlie Weeks and he lived in Iberia. His sons, Willie and Ned, dey run business in de court house. One of dem tax collector and de other lookin' after de land, and am de surveyor. Old missus named Mag Weeks.

"My pa named Dennis Joe and ma named Sabry Joe, and dey borned and raised on Weeks Island, in Louisiana. After dey old massa die, dey was 'vided up and falls to Massa Charlie Weeks, and dat where I borned, in Iberia on Bayou Teche.

"Massa Charlie, he live in de big brick house with white columns and everybody what pass dere know dat place. Dey have de great big tomb in corner de yard, where dey buries all dey folks, but buries de cullud folks back of de quarters. Dey's well fix in Louisiana, but not so good after dey come to Texas.

"Dey used to have big Christmas in Louisiana and lots of things for us, and a big table and kill hawgs and have lots to eat. But old Missus Mag, she allus treat me like her own chillen and make me set at de table with dem and eat.

"I was with Missus Mag on a visit to Mansfield when de war starts at six o'clock Sunday and go till six o'clock Monday. I went over dat battlefield and look at dem sojers dey kill. David McGill, a young massa, he git kill. He uncle, William Weeks, what done hired him to jine the army in he place, he goes to the battlefield to look for Massa David. De only way he knowed it was him, he have two gold eyeteeth with diamonds in dem. Some dem hurt sojers was prayin' and some cussin'. You could hear some dem hollerin', 'Oh, Gawd, help me.' Dey was layin' so thick you have to step over dem.

"I seed de sojers in Iberia. Dey take anythin' dey wants. Dey cotch de cow and kill it and eat it. Dey have de camp dere and dey jus' carry on. I used to go to de camp, 'cause dey give me crackers and sardines. But after dat Mansfield battle dey have up white flags and dey ain't no more war dere. But while it gwine on, I go to de camp and sometimes dem sojers give me meat and barbecue. Dey one place dere a lump salt big as dis house, and dey set fire to de house and left dat big lump salt. Anywhere dey camp dey burns up de house.

"I didn't know I'm free till a man say to me, 'Sissy, ain't you know you ain't got no more massa or missus?' I say, 'No, suh.' But I stays with dem till I git marry, and slep' right in dey house and nuss for dem. Dey give me de big weddin', too. De noter public in Iberia, he marry us. My husband name Henry Smith and dat when I'm fifteen year old. I so big-limb and fat den I bigger den what I is now.

"I ain't had no husband for a time. I can't cast de years, he been dead so long. Us have fifteen chillen, and seven livin' now.

"Sperrits? I used to see dem. I scart of dem. Sometime dey looks nat'ral and sometime like de shadow. Iffen dey look like de shadow, jus' keep on lookin' at dem till dey looks nat'ral. Iffen you walks 'long, dey come right up side you. Iffen you looks over you left shoulder, you see dem. Dey makes de air feel warm and you hair rise up, and sometime dey gives you de cold chills. You can feel it when dey with you. I set here and seed dem standin' in dat gate. Dey goes round like dey done when dey a-livin'. Some say dey can't cross water.

"I heared talk of de bad mouth. A old woman put bad mouth on you and shake her hand at you, and befo' de day done you gwine be in de acciden'.

"I seed de Klu Klux. Po' Cajuns and redbones, I calls dem. Dey ought to be sleepin'. One time I seed a man hangin' in de wood when I'n pickin' blackberries. His tongue hangin' out and de buzzards fly down on he shoulder. De breeze sot him to swingin' and de buzzards fly off. I tells de people and dey takes him down to bury. He a fine, young cullud man. I don't know why dey done it. Dat after peace and de Yankees done gone back home.

"I been here in Texas a good while, and it such a rough road it got my 'membrance all stir up. I never been to school, 'cause I bound out to work. I lives with my daughter and dis child here my grandchild. I can't 'member no more, 'cause my head ain't good as it used to be."

JOHN SNEED

John Sneed, born near Austin, Texas, does not know his age, but was almost grown when he was freed. He belonged to Dr. Sneed and stayed with him several years after Emancipation.

"I's borned on de old Sneed place, eight miles south of Austin, and my mammy was Sarah Sneed and pappy was Ike. Dey come from Tennessee and dere five boys and two gals. De boys am Dixie and Joe and Jim and Bob and me, and de gals name Katy and Lou. Us live in quarters what was log huts. Dere's one long, log house where dey spinned and weaved de cloth. Dere sixteen spinnin' wheels and eight looms in dat house and my job was turnin' one dem wheels when they'd thresh me out and git me to do it. Mos' all de clothes what de slaves and de white folks have was made in dat house.

"Mos' and usual de chillen sleept on de floor, unless with de old folks. De bedsteads make of pieces of split logs fasten with wooden pegs and rope criss-cross. De mattress make of shucks tear into strips with maybe a li'l cotton or prairie hay. You could go out on de prairie mos' any time and get 'nough grass to make de bed, and dry it 'fore it put in de tick. De white folks have bought beds haul by ox teams from Austin and feather beds.

"Dr. Sneed raise cotton and corn and wheat. Sometime five or six oxen hitch to de wagon and 25 or 30 wagons make what am call de wagon train. Dey haul cotton and corn and wheat to Port Lavaca what am de nearest shipping point. On de return trip, dey brung sugar and coffee and cloth and other things what am needed on de plantation. First time massa 'low me go with dat ox-train, I thunk I's growed.

"Dere a big gang of white and cullud chillen on de plantation but Dr. Sneed didn't have no chillen of he own. De neighbor white chillen come over dere and played. Us rip and play and fight and kick up us heels, and go on. Massa never 'low no whippin' of de chillen. He make dem pick rocks up and make fences out dem, but he didn't 'low no chillen work in de field till dey 'bout fourteen. De real old folks didn't work in de fields neither. Dey sot 'round and knit socks and mend de shoes and harness and stuff.

"Massa John mighty good to us chillen. He allus give us a li'l piece money every Sunday. When he'd git in he buggy to go to Austin to sell butter, de chillen pile in dat buggy and all over him so you couldn't see him and he'd hardly see to drive.

"Us had possum and rabbit and fish and trap birds for eatin'. Dere all kind wild green dem days. Us jus' go in de woods and git wild lettuce and mustard and leather-britches and polk salad and watercress, all us want to eat. Us kilt hawgs and put up de lard by de barrel. Us thresh wheat and take it to de li'l watermill at Barton Creek to grind. Dey'd only grind two bushel to de family, no matter how big dat family, 'cause dere so many folks and it such a small mill.

"Each family have de li'l garden and raise turnips and

cabbage and sweet 'taters and put dem in de kiln make from corn stalks and cure dem for winter eatin'. Us have homemake clothes and brogan shoes, come from Austin or some place. Us chillen wear shirt-tail till us 'bout thirteen.

"Massa live in de big two-story rock house and have he office and drug-store in one end de house. Missy Ann have no chillen so she 'dopt one from Tennessee, name Sally.

"Dere 'bout four or five hunerd acres and 'bout sixty slaves. Dey git up 'bout daylight and come from de field in time to feed and do de chores 'fore dark. After work de old folks sot 'round, fiddle and play de 'cordian and tell stories. Dat mostly after de crops laid by or on rainy days. On workin' time, dey usually tired and go to bed early. Dey not work on Saturday afternoon or Sunday, 'cept dey gatherin' de crop 'gin a rain. Old man Jim Piper am fiddler and play for black and white dances. On Sunday massa make us go to church. Us sing and pray in a li'l log house on de plantation and sometimes de preacher stop and hold meetin'.

"Massa John Sneed doctored from Austin to Lockhart and Gonzales and my own mammy he train to be midwife. She good pneumonia doctor and massa 'low her care for dem.

"On Christmas all us go to de big house and crowd 'round massa. He a li'l man and some black boys'd carry him 'round on dere shoulders. All knowed dey gwine git de present. Dere a big tree with present for everyone, white and black. Lots of eggnog and turkey and baked hawgs and all kind good things. Dere allus lots of white folks company at massa's house and big banquets and holidays and birthdays. Us like dem times, 'cause work slack and food heavy. Every las' chile have he birthday celebrate with de big cake and present and maybe de quarter in silver from old massa, bless he soul. Us play kissin' games and ring plays and one song am like dis:

> "'I'm in de well,
> How many feet?
> Five. Who'd git you out?'

"Iffen it a man, he choose de gal and she have to kiss him to git him out de well. Iffen a gal in de well, she choose a man.

"I well 'member de day freedom 'clared. Us have de tearin'-down dinner dat day. De niggers beller and cry and didn't want leave massa. He talk to us and say long as he live us be cared for, and us was. Dere lots of springs on he place and de married niggers pick out a spring and Massa Doctor give dem stuff to put up de cabin by dat spring, and dey take what dey have in de quarters. Dey want to move from dem slave quarters, but not too far from massa. Dey come to de big house for flour and meal and meat and sich till massa die. He willed every last one he slaves somethin'. Mos' of 'em git a cow and a horse and a pig and some chickens. My mammy git two cows and a pair horses and a wagon and 70 acres land. She marries 'gain when my daddy die and dat shif'less nigger she marry git her to sign some kind paper and she lose de land.

"My wife was Nanny Madeira and us have six chillen and five is livin'. I followed cattle till I's 'bout 26. I's went up de Chisholm Trail eight or nine times and druv for Massa Blocker and Jedge Brackenridge and others.

On one stampede I rode 24 hours straight and after we rounds up all de cattle, I goes to sleep under a tree. Dat day I has on a buckskin coat I in gen'ral wore and I feels somethin' grab dat coat and bite my side. I rouses up and sees de big panther draggin' me off to de thicket. I has de six-gun but I couldn't git to it. Every once in a while dat panther lay me down and sniff at my nose. I jes' hold de breath, 'cause if dat panther cotch me breathin' dat been de end of me. He drug me to some bushes and den goes off a li'l way and give de yell. Dat yell make me turn cold, 'cause it sound jes' like a man screamin'. Den dat cat dug a shallow hole. I eases out my old gun, takes careful aim and den says, 'Thank you, old man,' and he turns to look at me and I shoots him right 'tween he eyes. After 'while, dat cat's mate and cub come runnin', 'cause he yell for dem, and I kilt dem, too.

John Sneed

"'Nother time, I seed de panther a-draggin' a white man off and I slips up jes' as de cat seizes him and shoots dat cat. Us have to run dat man down and cotch him, 'cause he scared stiff when dat dead cat fall on him.

"Some time after dat I works for a man what freights supplies 'round Austin and I's one de drivers. Us start in September with sev'ral six-wheel wagons, 'nough to las' a town de year, and not git back to Austin till January. Sometimes de mud so bad it take six oxen to pull de wagon out.

"One time us movin' and stampedin' de bunch cattle and me and my brother gits los' from de rest and was los' three days and nights. All us eat am parched corn. De grass nearly waist high to a man and us scoop out de hole in de ground and cut off tops de grass and weeds and make de fire. Den us drap de corn on de fire and parch it. De woods full wild animals and panthers and wolves. De wolves de worst. Dey slip up on us to git de chicken us has with us. At last us come to a house and finds us folks."

MARIAH SNYDER

Mariah Snyder, 89, was born in Mississippi, a slave of Sam Miller, who brought her to Texas when she was five. Since Mariah's second husband died, twenty-two years ago, she has earned her living by washing and cooking. Now too old to do much, she is cared for by her only living daughter, with the aid of a $10.00 monthly pension.

"I's borned in Mississippi. Yes, sar. I 'longed to Massa Miller and he name am Sam, and my name am Mariah. My pappy was Weldon and my mammy, Ann. Massa Sam fotches all us to Texas when I's jes' five year old and we come in wagons and hossback. He done buy my mammy and pappy in the slave market, so I don't know nothin' 'bout none my other 'lations.

"Massa Sam live in a great big, ceiled house, and had plenty land and niggers. The quarters was logs and any kind beds we could git. We wore lowell clothes and I never seed no other kind of dress till after surrender. We et meat and collards and cornbread and rough grub, and they biled all the victuals in a big, black pot what hung on a rack in the kitchen fireplace. We had red russet, flat shoes and no stockin's, but in winter we made wool panties to wear on our legs.

"Missy was name Patsy and she was purty good, and

Massa Sam was purty good, too. He'd whip us if we needed it. He'd pull off our clothes and whip in the field. But he wouldn't 'low the driver to whip us if we didn't need it. No, sar. And he wouldn't have no patterrollers on the place.

"The driver come round and woke everybody up and had 'em in the field by daybreak. I's seed a whole field of niggers abreast, hoein'. The rows of cotton was so long you couldn't make but one 'fore dinnertime. I driv the gin, what was run by two mules. The cotton was wropped in baggin' and tied with ropes. It was a long time after 'fore I seed cotton tied with steel like they bales it now.

"I seed plenty niggers whipped while I driv that gin. They tied the feets and hands and rawhided 'em good. They tied a bell on one woman what run away all the time. They locks it round her head.

"I seed lots of niggers put on the block and bid off and carry away in chains. One woman name Venus raises her hands and hollers, 'Weigh dem cattle,' whilst she's bein' bid off.

"The big folks dances all night Sat'day. That's all the fun we had. We used to sing

> "I'm in a lady's garden, I'm in a lady's garden,
> So let me out. I'm sufferin' for water and wine.

"The slaves most allus sings whilst theys workin' in the field, and one song was

> "When I's here you calls me honey,
> When I's gone you honies everybody.

or

"The raccoon am de funny thing,
Ramblin' round in de dark.

"Massa Sam have a cullud man what give us our ABC's. I still got mine, but didn't never git no further.

Mariah Snyder

"Massa Sam git kilt 'fore the war. A mule throwed him. He had plenty good hosses but allus rid a mule. He come in from a neighbor's one day and the mule throwed him on a stob 'fore he got to the house. We heared a hollerin' down the road, but didn't pay no 'tention, 'cause they's allus all kind racket gwine on. Fin'ly somebody say, 'That sound like a man,' and we goes down there and it was massa. 'Fore he die he calls all the cullud chillen to him and shakes hands and tells 'em to be good.

"We 'longs to he son, Ruben, then, and stays with him three years after surrender. Lordy me! How I hates to think of 'em talkin' 'bout that war! Young missy cry a whole week, 'cause she fear her men folks gwine git kilt. They did, too. Her two boys, George and Frank, gits kilt, and heap of the neighbors boys gits kilt, too.

"Fin'ly us leaves Massa Ruben and goes to Shreveport and I marries Snyder. The 'Progo' Marshal marries us. We raises two gals and I lives with Mary. Snyder died twenty-two years ago and all them years I made a livin' washin' and ironin' and cookin', up to six years ago. I gits a pension from the gov'ment now and it am $10.00 a month. It's mighty good of the white folks to take care of this old nigger, but I'd rather work, only I ain't able no more."

PATSY SOUTHWELL

Patsy Southwell, 83, was born in Jasper Co., Texas. She has lived on or near the old plantation all her life. Her master was Bill Trailor.

"My name Patsy Southwell and I lives at Rock Hill. I been livin' on dat plantation all my life, but not allus in the very same place. I think the house was move and 'nother builded.

"My pappy was John Redd and he 'longed to Bill Trailor and he brung here from Virginny. Mammy's name Rose Redd and she a yaller nigger, come from South Carolina and maybe she white and Indian, too. My brothers call Dennis, George, William, and Charles and dey all dead.

"We all live in the quarters and massa a tol'able good one 'sidering others what cut and slashes bad. Pappy and mammy work in the field and dey send pappy and he sons off six months at the time, over to Alexandria, to make salt.

"My brothers hunt all the time and brung in deer and wild turkey, so we has lots to eat. We has butter and milk and honey and pappy allus have he li'l garden patch.

"We wears slip homespun dress make outten cloth from us loom. I never have shoes and us has no Sunday clothes. Massa was tol'ably good to the old folks and not so mean to the chillen. He wasn't no barbarian like some what whip the slaves every Monday mornin' befo' dey starts to work.

"Massa plantation have fifteen hunnerd acre in it and he didn't have 'nough slaves so they works awful hard. I seed 'em hit my mammy five hunnerd licks and my pappy six hunnerd. Pappy have run 'way and been gone long time and they cotch him in de water in the Neches River. He have meat and stuff and they say mammy feedin' him, but I think it the other way. I think he gittin' and sendin' her stuff.

"The white folks has the big church with the bar 'cross it and the cullud folks sit behin' the bar. If any wants to jine us tell massa and he tell the preacher, and he old man Southwell. They baptise at the mill pond.

"I marries Jerry Southwell and us git marry at home. Jerry wears the black suit and I wears the dotted white Swiss dress with the overskirt.

"When freedom breaks and massa say we free, we goes to the Haynes' place and my pappy farms for hisself. We gits on better den in slavery days and after 'while pappy buys him some land and den we all right. Me and my husban', we stays on with pappy awhile, but we gits our own farm and farm all us life."

LEITHEAN SPINKS

Leithean Spinks, 82, was born a slave to Fay Thompson, in Rankin County, Mississippi. Soon after Leithean's birth, Mr. Thompson moved to E. Feliciana Parish, Louisiana. Leithean was happy in slave days, and stayed with her master two years after she was freed. She lives at 2600 Merrick St., Fort Worth, Texas.

"Does I look old 'nough to be birthed in slavery? I's eighty-two years old and mammy had it right there in de Bible, marked when I's birthed, in 1855. I's birthed in Mississippi but a little while after, massa goes to Louisiana, over in East Feliciana Parish, and when I's old 'nough to 'member, we'uns am there, 'twixt New Roads and Jackson, right near the Mississippi River.

"Massa Thompson had a awful big plantation and more'n 300 cullud folks, and three rows of cabins 'bout two blocks long, and 'bout one family to a cabin. No floors in dem cabins, you stands on dirt, and de furniture am something you knows ain't there. Why, man, there am jus' benches to sit on and a homemake table and bunks. Dere am de fireplace but all de main cookin' am done in de big cookin' shed, and old Mammy Dice done it, with four to holp her.

"De bell am rung when meal time comes and all de slaves lines up, with their pans and cups and passes de service table, and de food am put on dere pans and milk in de cup. Dat de one time massa could allus 'pend on de niggers. When de bell say, 'Come and git it,' all us am there. Us takes de food to de cabins and eats it.

"Dis old nigger come near gwine to Glory once when mammy am gone to de cook shed. How 'twas am dis-a-way. She latches de door on de outside to keep us three chillen in de cabin, my sis and brudder and me. Well, in dem days, us uses tallow candles for light and pine knots when candles am short. Mammy lights de pine knot befo' she leaves and after she am gone, it falls off de hook and hits de ground and rolls a couple feet under de bunk. There am straw in de tick and right off de whole shebang am on fire. There am three of us with de door latch and all de grown-ups in de cook shed. Us hollers and yells but it am no use, and de hollerin' don't last long, 'cause de smoke gittin' thick. De fire am spreadin' fast and de bunks starts burnin'. Us am huddle togedder, skeert plumb out our wits and chokin' and coughin'.

"Den my brudder gits de idea and he grabs de big spoon and de iron poker and starts diggin' de dirt from under de log next de door. De smoke ain't so bad next de ground, and did yous ever see de dog diggin' in de rabbit hole? Dat how us digs, and seems it never gwine come a hole. Finally, a hole busted through and lets in fresh air, and den us dig some more, and it am big 'nough for my little sis to crawl through. Den us dig some more and I crawls out and my brudder starts but he gits he head outside and his shoulders wedges and there he am, stuck. Us pull and pull, but nary a inch could us budge him. He try to back up but he shirt caught on a knot and he can't do dat. So us runs for de cook shed and yells, 'Mammy, de cabin on fire.' Everybody starts to holler, 'Fire,' and mammy busts in de door and yanks brudder out dat hole, and he am sweatin' like a latherin' mare. After dey puts de fire out with de water buckets, mammy say, 'When sis gits out, why didn't she unlatch de door?' 'Cause de 'citement, us never think of dat!

"Us have plenty hawg meat and veg'tables and butter and 'lasses and honey. De food ain't short no time 'round massa, 'cause he say niggers works better when dey feeds good. De mammies leaves de babies in de nursery durin' de day and dem chillen am take good care of and has lots of milk and am all fat like hawgs.

"In de mornin' when de bell ring, everybody goes to work, but I is little and does de chores and am gap tender. De cattle am 'lowed to run where dey wants, here, there and all over. Fences am 'round de fields and yards and there am gates to go through, but us calls dem gaps. It am my job to open and close dem, 'cause somebody allus wantin' to drive or walk through dem gaps.

"MY sis am de fly chaser. She has de big fan make from de tail feathers of de peacock. 'Twas awful purty thing. She stands 'round de white folks and shoo off de flies.

"Massa Fay ain't hard on he cullud folks. He works dem steady but don't drive dem. Lots de slaves goes fishin' in de river on Saturday afternoon and Sunday, and dey cotches plenty fish.

"Us has parties and singin' and dancin' and fiddle music. Oh, Lawdy! How lonesome I gits when I thinks 'bout dem days, and de music and singin'. Sometimes 'bout a hunerd sings to once and dat sound purty and jus' go all through me.

Leithean Spinks

"For runnin' off am de only hard whuppin's massa give. De run-off am tie to de log and massa lay de whuppin' on he back. De plantation am near de river and dere am lots of caves and cliffs to hide in. Massa cotch de run-offs with de nigger hounds and if he don't, dey git hongry and sneaks back. Only one gits clear away.

"One Sunday mornin' 'bout ten o'clock, massa have de bell ring and calls all us to de front gallery and makes de talk. He say, 'I's happy to tell yous is free and, 'cording to de law, yous am all citizens. Dem what wants to stay with me I'll pay de wages or dey can work on shares.' He gives us all de paper, with de name and age and where us am birthed. Me and mammy stays two years after freedom. I marries Sol Pleasant in 1872 and us has two chillen. Us sep'rate in 1876. De trouble am, he wants to be de boss of de job and let me do de work. I 'cides I don't need no boss, so I transports him, and says, 'Nigger, git out of here and don't never come back. If you comes back, I'll smack you down.'

"In 1876 I marries Frank Spinks and us has eight chlllen and he dies in 1930. All dem eight chillen lives here and I's livin' with one of dem, Mrs. Covy Kelly. 'Tain't many years befo' old Gabriel blow he horn, and I's waitin' for him."

GUY STEWART

Guy Stewart, 87, 209 Austin Ave., Ft. Worth, was born Nov. 26, 1850, a slave of Jack Taylor, who also owned Guy's parents, 3 brothers and 3 sisters. They lived in Mansfield Parish, La. Stewart started work in the fields at seven years, and remained with his owner three years after he was freed. He then moved onto his own farm where he lived until 1898, when he moved to Fort Worth.

"Yas, suh, I'se an ol' slave and I'se 'bout 11 years ol' when de War starts. My marster am Jack Taylor and my family belongs to him.

"I 'members de war well, 'cause we'uns hears shootin' and see soldiers. Dey comes to marster's place and takes hosses and vittals. One time dey wants some of de niggers for to help fix for de battle. Dere am heap of 'citement and de marster's 'fraid de battle come too close. He say, 'It's too close for saftment.' And he say, 'Put dis and dat away so de soldier cain't find it.'

"I starts work long 'fore dat, when I'se seven, in de cotton and co'n field. I just peddles 'round first. Marster sho' am good to us and so good dat de other white folks calls us de 'free niggers.'

"We'uns have cabins for to live in and sleep in bunks

with straw ticks on 'em. We'uns has lots to eat, all we wants. And we'uns have all de clothes we needs.

"Sho, we went to church with de marster. Dey tol' us 'bout Heaven and de devil and sich. But dey never 'lows us to have books in de hands. Dey says it wasn' good for us to larn readin' or writin.' "We'uns has lots of music on dat place 'cause de marster, he am de good fiddler and he learns some of us niggers to play de fiddle and de banjo. We gits together and has de music, sing and dance. If I thinks 'bout dem days now, I can see we'uns dancin' and hear de singin' of dem ol' songs, sich like Ol' Black Joe and Swanee River. Iffen I thinks too much 'bout dem days, tears comes in dis ol' nigger's eyes. Dem were de happy days of my life. In dem days, we'uns not know what am money, never have any. What for we'uns need it? I'se more happy den, dan I been since, with money.

"De marster am scart for to lose all de hosses and everything, 'cause dey takes it for de army man, so he gits to thinkin' 'bout movin' to Texas. De war warn't over when he goes to Texas and takes all us niggers with him. De roads dem days am not so good. No bridges over de rivers, 'cept de bigges' ones. Lots of times we'uns has to push for help de hosses pull de wagons outta de mudhole, and we'uns is over a month gettin' to Williams County. De marster rents de land dere and we stays for one crop, and den we all goes to Travis County, whar marster settle for to raise de wheat.

"When freedom comes, de marster says we'uns has to work for wages and buy all de food and de clothes and everything dat we'uns gits. Dat's not so easy. At first he pays me $5.00 a month and den pays me $10.00 de month. After three years I quits and rents a farm and works for myself, I gits married in 1877 and my wife dies in 1915. We'uns has one chile. In 1898 I comes to Fort Worth and gits me a job in de woodyard and sich.

"White man, I sho' likes for to see dat ol' plantation down in Louisiana and it would do dis ol' darky good. I sits here and thinks of de marster and de good times. And de fishin down dere! Is dere good fishin'? De folks here don' know what am fishin'.

"You has dis nigger thinkin' heaps 'bout de ol' plantation and de good times. If I don' stop talkin' 'bout dat, I gits to cryin'."

WILLIAM STONE

William Stone was born in a covered wagon, on the way from Alabama to Texas, about 1863. Though he was too small to remember slave days, he does recall many things told him by his parents and other ex-slaves. William lives in Mart, Texas.

"My parents done told me where I's borned. It am in a covered wagon on de way from Alabama to Texas, two years 'fore freedom. Old Marse, Lem Stone, he left Alabama for Texas, where de war not so bad, and brung some he slaves with him. He done lost so much in Alabama, Yankees burnin' he house and cotton and killin' he stock, he want to git 'way from dere.

"First he come to Rusk County, den goes back to Shreveport and stays till freedom. Pappy and mammy was Louis and Car'line Stone. I lived in Louisiana till I's growed.

"Mammy and pappy done told me all 'bout de old plantation. It am hundreds of acres of land, part worked and part jus' timber and pasture. It was near Montgomery, and dey raised more cotton den anything else, but had some corn and peas and cane. Dey made sorghum and ribbon cane 'lasses and had boilin' vats for sugar, too.

"De soldiers come through. Dey named, Yankees. Dey

make mammy cook somethin' to eat and den kilt all de hawgs and took de meat with dem, and burn de barn and house. Old Marse had pens to put cotton in, hid way out in de bresh. Dey picked it in gunny sacks and hides it, and slips it out to de gin by night and tries to sell it 'fore dem Yankees finds it and burns it.

"Mammy say dey all went to church and had to drive four horses when de roads muddy in winter and sand deep in summer. Dey allus carry dinner and stay all day. Den in de evenin', after de niggers had dey preachin', dey all go home. Sometimes a preacher come out to de plantation and hold church for de white folks in de mornin' and in de evenin' for de niggers, out under a big oak tree.

"De Lawd say iffen us trusts him and help to be good he gwine make our path straight. Dis was true in de days of den, 'cause our white folks tooken care of us, befo' dey was freedom and sech. Now, us gittin' old, and gits de old age pension when us too old to work.

"I works all up and down de old river when I's growed. De plantations has long staple cotton. Dey raise sugar cane and dere be twenty wagons haulin' cane to de boilin' mills. We was happy to do dat work, 'cause we knowed it mean us have plenty 'lasses in winter. Lawdy, I wish I knowed I could have all de 'lasses and bread I wanted dis winter! Dem was good times, Lawd! Us sing dis song:

> "'We'll stick to de hoe till de sun go down,
> We'll rise when de rooster crow,
> And go to de field where de sunshine hot,
> To de field where de sugar cane grow.
> Yes, chilluns, we'll all go.'

"I can jes' see dem long rows of cotton and niggers drivin' de oxen and mules. I know 'nother song:

> "Nigger mighty happy when he layin' by de corn,
> Nigger mighty happy when he hear dat dinner horn;
> But he more happy when de night come on,
> Dat' sun's a'slantin', as sho's you born!
> Dat old cow's a shakin' dat great big bell,
> And de frogs tunin' up, 'cause de dew's done fell.'

"Dat jes' after freedom. Dey have plantations and overseers like slavery, but most de overseers niggers, and dey didn't whip you den. On Saturday night de overseer pay us, mostly in rations. He give us five, maybe ten pounds rations of meat, and a peck or two or meal, and some coffee and 'lasses.

> "'Dat ration day come once a week,
> Old massa rich as Gundy.
> But he give 'lasses all de week,
> And buttermilk for Sunday.
>
> "'Old massa give a pound of meat,
> I et it all on Monday;
> Den I et 'lasses all de week,
> And buttermilk for Sunday.'

"All dis was down on de Mississippi bottom. Old Man River was sho' purty in de fall, when dem wild geeses come in droves and de blossoms red and yaller. De fogs come hang over and chills and fever gits started. De woman sot by de fire piecin' quilts and spinnin' thread, and de old men weave cotton baskets and chair bottoms, and de young men work on da levees, so dey hold Old Man River back when he start prowlin' round 'gain.

William Stone

"Floods come down, no matter what time of year. One day Old Man River be runnin' 'long, jes' as peaceful and quiet, and everybody happy. Everybody meet de boats at de landin'. Den way in de night you wake up and hear a roarin' like thunder and dat river be on a tear. Folks know he am in de ugly mood, and starts movin' to higher ground. Everybody what have a wagon and mule gits out. Some jes' gits to de levee. It look like my folks told me when dey run from de Yankees, only dis time it's de river. Old Man River sho' treach'ous. After he go on one he rarin' and tearin' spells, den he gwine be so peaceful and quiet like. Look like he try to make up for he meanness.

"I gits married and moves clost to de Trinity River, and stays till my family done raised. Dey has free schools in Texas den. I works in de sawmill and dere so much wild game us can eat easy. Dem days on de Mississippi bottom is like a dream, but when I hears talk 'bout Old Man River, I can dem big waters roarin' down."

YACH STRINGFELLOW

Yach Stringfellow, 90, was born a slave of Frank Hubert, in Brenham, Texas. His memory is poor and, though he recalled a good many incidents of slavery days, he had little to say about his life from 1865 to the present. He now lives in Watt, Texas.

"I'll be ninety-one years old next May, and I was borned in Brenham. My massa and missus was Frank Hubert and Sarah Ann Hubert. My daddy come from de old Africa and was tall and straight as a arrow. He was sold to a man what tooked him to California in de gold rush in 1849 and me and mammy stays with Massa Hubert. Dat how come my name ain't de same as massa have.

"I got so much misery in de head I can't 'member like I should. But I know us live in little log houses all kind of group together, and us eat in a long lean-to builded on to the big house. Us chillen had a long, scooped-out dish on a split log table. What we had to eat was dumped in dat trough and us ate it like slop. But it sho' taste good when you been huntin' for eggs or calves or gittin' in chips or breakin' bresh.

"When I's big 'nough I carries water, sometimes from de spring and sometimes from de deep well. Dere danger a little child fall in and drown and massa, he say niggers too valu'ble to risk dem dat way. It was hard work to tote water for niggers workin', 'cause allus somebody hollerin' for de water. I had to trot down de slippery bank through de thorns to de spring or pull de heavy sweep to git it out de well, and carry two buckets most de time.

"Us cut two saplin's de right size to fasten together at de end and stick dem in holes in de wall, to make de bed. Us use lace cowhide strings or any kind rope across de poles to hold de bed up. Den put hay or corn shucks and a little cotton in de ticks.

"Us eat bacon and cornbread and greens, but de white folks had more'n better. Dey didn't have to eat string victuals like us; us have to eat something to stick to de ribs. Right 'bout de time dis state come to be de United States, and de Mexicans raisin' de old billy, us cook most usual on de fireplace and have ovens by de side to make bread, and cranes for de pots.

"Us slaves used pine torches and sometimes a little bit of candle. De women make all de candles demselves for de white folks. Us didn't need much light at night, 'cause us tired after de long day, workin' from can see to can't see, and us git in de bed early.

"I wore shirt tail till I's fourteen, den de homespun britches and shirt. My weddin' suit was de dark jeans and I was fix up fine as any nigger on de plantation. She wore white and massa fix supper and git de fiddler and all sich.

"Massa have John to oversee, and he sho' de stepper. He be every place you didn't think he gwine come. He have de big, boom voice and allus slingin', and wail, 'Look along, black man, look along, dere trouble comin' sho'.' Iffen de black boy or woman lyin' in de corn row, dey git up quick and be mighty bust right soon, 'cause dat black snake whip reach for dem. Dey scramble deyself together and be de busiest in de bunch by time John git dere.

Yach Stringfellow

"In de long winter days de men sat round de fire and whittle wood and make butter paddles and troughs for de pigs and sich, and ax handles and hoe handles and box traps and figure-four traps. Dey make combs to git de wool clean for de spinnin'. Us take de long strip of leather and put wire in it and bend dem so dey stay, den cut dem comb-like teef and dere you are.

"Come Christmas us slaves have de big dinner and eat all day and dance till nex' mornin'. Some de niggers from near plantations git dey passes and come jine us. Course dey a drap egg nog round and candy for de chillen. De white folks have dey big carriage full of visitors and big goin's on dey come to from miles round. Us didn't have no money, but didn't have no place to go to spend it, neither.

"At night, us sat round de fire sometimes and de women sew and knit and de men whittle and told things. Dey talk 'bout charms and sich. You gwine have lots of luck iffen you cotch de rabbit in de graveyard on de dark of de moon and cut off he hind leg and wear it. Iffen you chews de piece of shoe-string root, jus' you ask anybody a favor and you sho' gwine git it."

BERT STRONG

Bert Strong was born in 1864, a slave of Dave Cavin. He and his mother remained in the service of the Cavin family for ten years after they were freed. Bert has farmed in Harrison County all his life and now lives alone on Long's Camp Road, twelve miles northeast of Marshall. He is supported by a $15.00 per month pension.

"I been livin' here all my life. I was birthed a year and more 'fore the war stopped and 'longed to old Dave Cavin. All my folks 'longed to him over in Montgomery, in Alabama. Massa Dave buyed my mammy's papa off a 'baccy farm in Richmond, in Virginny. I heared Massa Dave say he done come to Texas 'cause he heared in Alabama this was a rich country—hawgs walkin' round with a knife in they back and you could shake money off the trees. His folks and 'bout thirty slaves cone to Texas in wagons. They was on the road three months.

"I heared my grand-people tell 'bout holpin' run the Indians out of Texas. Big Lake, on Caddo Lake, was jus' a small kind of stream them days. My grandpa was name Gloster and he died at a hunerd five years.

"Massa Cavin had 'bout four hunerd acres and builded us all good quarters with chimnies and fireplaces, and good beds and plenty food. I's too little to know all this 'fore the war, but my folks stayed with massa ten years after freedom and things was jus' the same as in slave times, only they got a little money, so I can 'member.

"My grandma was cook and there was plenty wild game, turkey and deer and pigeon and rabbits and squirrels. I 'member once they's grumblin' 'bout what they have to eat and old massa comes to the quarters and say, 'What you fussin' 'bout? They's a gallon good potlicker in the pot." I's raise on greens and pork and potlicker and 'taters and ash-cake. Dat am good food, too. I ain't never hope to see no better food dan dat.

"Massa give he slaves two sets clothes a year and one pair 'bachelor' brogan shoes with brass toes. The white folks larnt us Negroes to read and write, at night and on Sunday, and we could go to church. We had our own preacher, and massa let us have fun'rals when a slave died. They wasn't no undertakers then. They jus' made the coffin and planed the boards and lined it with black cloth. The white folks and the cullud folks, too, was put 'way nice on our place.

"They was a overseer a while, but massa fires him for cuttin' and slashin' he niggers. He made my uncle Freeman overlooker. We is heared slaves on farms close by hollerin' when they git beat. Some the neighbors works they hands till ten at night and weighed the last weighin' by candles. If the day's pickin' wasn't good 'nough, they beat them till it a pity.

"Christmas was the big time. Massa kilt the hawg or beef and sometimes a mutton, and give the slaves the big dinner. Us all hang the stockin' up on massa's gallery and it was a run to see what we'd git. He give the chillen toys and apples and the big folks somethin' to wear. He'd 'low the chillen to have candy pullin' Saturday nights and the growed folks parties. My cousin, Tom, was songster and call the plays at all the dances, and they turned 'cordin' to what he'd sing.

"When young massa went to war they calls all the slaves to tell him good-bye. They blowed the horn. He come home two times on a furlough and says, 'I's smellin' and seein' the Devil.' Then the nex' time he come home he say, 'Las' time I tells you 'bout smellin' the Devil. I's smellin' and seein' Hell now.' When the war am over, he come home and say to old massa, 'Ain't you read the 'lamation to you niggers yet?' Massa say he hasn't, and young massa blowed the horn and calls us all up and tells us we's free as he is and could work for who we please, but he like us to stay till the crop am out. He say he'd hire us and make a contrac'. Me and my mammy stays ten years, 'cause they so good it ain't no use to leave. One of the young massas am livin' here now, Mr. Tom, and I goes to see him.

Bert Strong

"I stays with mammy till I marries and then farms for myself. That all I ever done and I'd be doin' it now if I was able. I raises two boys but they am both dead now.

"I votes once in the county 'lection and once in the

president 'lection. I think any man should vote, but it ain't 'tended for women to vote.

"Mos' the young niggers am gwine to Hell. They don't 'preciate things. They has lots more'n we ever did. They can go to school and all, but they don't 'preciate it."

EMMA TAYLOR

Emma Taylor, 89, was born a slave of the Greer family, in Mississippi. She and her mother were sold to a Texas man, whose name Emma has forgotten. Emma lives with one of her children, in Tyler, Texas.

"My maw and paw lived in Mississippi, and belonged to Marse Greer. Dat dere name, too. All the slaves tooken dere master's name, 'cause dey hadn't no use for a name, nohow.

"De first thing I 'members is followin' my maw in the cotton patch. She allus went ahead, pickin' cotton, and made a clean place with her sack draggin' on the ground. But de first work I ever done was feed de chickens and geese and shell corn to feed dem.

"Us nigger chillen couldn't play with de white chillen. De worstest whippin' I ever got was fer playin' with a doll what belonged to one marse's chillen. I 'members it yet and I ain't never seed a doll purty as dat doll was to me. It was make out a corncob with arms and legs what moved and a real head, with eyes and hair and mouth painted on. It had a dress out of silk cloth, jist like one my missus weared when she went to meetin'. Dat li'l gal done leave de doll under de tree, but missus found me playin' with it and whipped me hard.

"We lived in a cabin in de back field 'hind de big

house, one room and a shed room, where maw done all de cookin' for de whole family. I had three brothers and three sisters, all dead, I supposes. Dey all older'n what I was. We cooked on a fireplace, and a big pot hanged on poles over de fire and de bread cook on dat fire in a skillet what was made of two pieces of iron, turn up all round. We puts de dough in one and turns de other one over it, den buries it in de coals a few minutes till it brown on de top and bottom. It was good, jist as good as nowadays, baked in a oven. Our beds was made out of straw and old rags, but we kept warm sleepin' a whole lot in one bed in winter, but we slept outside in summer.

"I was sold one time. Marse, he gittin' old and 'cide he didn't need so many slaves, so he have de sale and a man come and put us all up on a big platform. We pulls off nearly all our clothes, so as to show how big we was, and he 'gins hollerin' 'bout who gwineter buy, who gwineter buy. I was scart and thunk I has to leave maw, so I 'gins hollerin' jist as loud as he does. He turn 'round and say, 'Shut up, you li'l coon, you. I can't hear nothin'.' I hides my face in maw's apron and didn't know no more till we's all loaded in a wagon and starts to de new home. We gits dere and is give new clothes and shoes, de first ones I ever had on and it taken me a long time to larn to wear dem things on my feet.

"Us niggers has to git up at four in de mornin', and work, work till us can't see no more. Den dey work at night. De men chops wood and hauls poles to build fences and make wood, and de women folks has to spin four cuts of thread every night and make all de clothes. Some has to card cotton to make quilts and some weave and knits stockin's. Marse give each one a chore to do at night and iffen it warn't did when we went to bed, we's whipped. One time I falls plumb asleep befo' I finishes shellin' some corn, but I didn't git a bad whippin' dat time.

"Sometimes de niggers danced and played de fiddle and us chillen played in de yard. We could stay up all night dem times, but had to work next day, and hardly ever stayed up all night. Dat durin' harvest or at Christmas time.

"All de victuals was issued out by de overseer and he give 'nough for one week, den iffen us eat it all up too soon, it am jist go without. Lots of times, I went down to de 'tato patch a long time after everybody am in bed, and stole 'tatoes, so we wouldn't be hungry next day. I allus covered de hole up good and never did git cotched. De dogs got after me one time, but I put pepper in dey eyes and dey stopped. I allus carried pepper with me.

Emma Taylor

"I marries when I's fifteen, not so long befo' I'm free. Nigger men didn't git no license to marry dey gals den. Dey jist picked her out and asked marse, and iffen he 'grees, dey's married. But iffen he don't want it, dat man has to find heself 'nother gal. De men what lived on 'nother plantation couldn't see dere wives but onct every two weeks. Marse buyed my husban', Rube Taylor, and he come to live with me.

"One day marse say we's all free and we has a big celebration, eatin' and dancin'. But we near all stayed on his place for a long time after day. He paid us thirty-five cents de day and let us live in de same old houses.

"After we done left him, we jist drifts 'round, workin' for white folks, till we manages to git a farm. Rube done died a long time back, and I lives with my baby child."

MOLLIE TAYLOR

Mollie Taylor, 84, was born a slave to John Wilson, at Campbell, Texas. After she was freed, Mollie moved with her family to an adjoining farm which they worked on shares. Mollie now lives at 522 Seaton St., Fort Worth, Texas.

"Now den, I's no record of when I's born and just what de white folks tells me is all I knows. I'll be 84 this coming October, but just what day I don't know. I's born on Massa John Wilson's farm at Campbell, Texas and him owned my father and mother and 'bout 20 more slaves. Dere was 'bout four or five chillen in we'uns family. My father died and I don't 'member much 'bout him, but his name was Anson Wilson and my mother name was Hattie Wilson. We'uns gits de name from de massa.

"Us slaves lived in log houses back of massa's house, and they was two and three-room houses with dirt floors and de rock fireplace and just holes for windows. De flies come in de door and go out de window, but most of 'em stayed in de house. Dere was no furniture like am today. No, suh, it was homemake stuff. De bunks was built 'gainst de wall and full of straw or hay and de tables was made of split logs. Dere was de cook room and de eatin' room where all de slaves meals cooked and they ate, 'tween de slaves quarters and de massa's house.

"Massa Wilson, him feed us purty good, with de cornmeal and 'lasses and plenty coffee and milk. We has white flour once a week and massa git de sugar by de barrel. De slaves could have dere own gardens and dey raised most dere vegetables. All de chillen ate out of de wooden trough with wooden spoons. It was a sight to watch them, day just like de bunch of pigs.

"De overseer, him ring de bell 'bout half past four in de mornin' and everybody what work go to de fields. De massa purty reason'ble with de work and didn't whip much. On Sundays de old slaves goes to de church and de chillen plays.

"When war come dere lots of soldiers allus ridin' by de place, all deck out in de uniform with big, shiny buttons on de coat. When us chillen seed dem we took to de woods.

"After freedom we'uns moves to de next farm and works and I stays dere with my family till I's 'bout 25 year old, and den I marries Tom Gould and move to McLennan County. But he so mean I didn't stay with him very long, and 'bout six months of his foolishness and I ups and leaves him. After two years I marries George Taylor and I lives with dat man for 12 years and took 'nough of his foolishness, so I leaves him. I's had four chillen but Tom Gould nor George Taylor wasn't de father of any of 'em. No, suh, I just found dem chillen."

JAKE TERRIELL

Jake Terriell, born a slave of Felix Terriell in Raleigh, South Carolina, does not know his age. He was grown and married at the close of the Civil War, so is probably in the 90's. He lives in Madisonville, Texas.

"Pappy and mammy was called Tom and Jane and they's cotched in Africy and brung to America and sold. My brother was called James and my sisters Lucindy and Sally. Massa Felix Terriell owned me and pappy and mammy but when I's still a chile he done give me to he son, Massa Dalton Terriell.

"My papy was de wild man and he so wild Massa Felix have to keep him locked up at night and in de chains by day to keep him from runnin' off. He had to wear de chains in de field and den he couldn't run fast.

"Massa Dalton growed de tobaccy. He was a good massa and give me de nickel and de dime sometime and I'd buy candy. He have lots of slaves and de cook fix our grub in big old skillets. We allus have de cornbread and de syrup and some meat. I likes possum cooked with sweet 'taters.

"Missy Mary try larn me read and write but I never did care for de book larnin'. Massa wake us 'bout four o'clock with de great iron and hammer and us work long as us could see.

"Massa didn't have to whip us but I seed pappy whip, with de rawhide with nine tails. He got thirty-nine licks and every lick, it brung de blood.

"I seed slaves sold and you has heared cattle bawl when de calves took from de mammy and dat de way de slaves bawls. When massa sell de slave he make 'em wash up and grease de face good and stand up straight and he fatten 'em jus' like you do hawgs to sell. I had de good massa. He was good to black debbils, what he call us niggers. Us could rest when us git to de quarters or go by de big tank and take de bath, and every Saturday night us git de holiday and have banjo and tin pan beatin' and dance. On Christmas massa kilt de big hawg and us fix it jus' like us wants and have big dinner.

"Massa have doctor when us sick. He say us too val'ble. If us sold us brung 'bout $1,000. Old mammy could fix de charm and git us well. She gather bark and make de tea. Most us sickness chill and fever. Sometime a slave git leg broke and massa say he no more 'count and finish him up with de club.

"Massa nearly kilt in de fightin' and he had he doctor write missy to set us free. I had two wives and missy said I couldn't keep but one, so I takes Mary and us starts out for Texas, a-foot. Us most starved to death 'fore us got here and then us have hard time. But dere plenty wild meat and dat what us lived on three, four year. Us had two chillen and den she dies and I marry a half-Indian gal and she died. Us jus' 'greed to live together in dem days, no weddin'. Then I marries Lucie Grant and us have 11 chillen and de preacher calls us man and wife. I's pappy to 17 chillen and I don't know how many grandchillen. Lucie say more'n a hun'erd."

J.W. TERRILL

J.W. Terrill was born in DeSoto Parish, Louisiana, and is about 100 years old. His master was his father. He now lives in Madisonville, Texas.

"My father took me away from my mother when at age of six weeks old and gave me to my grandmother, who was real old at the time. Jus' befo' she died she gave me back to my father, who was my mammy's master. He was a old batchelor and run saloon and he was white, but my mammy was a Negro. He was mean to me.

"Finally my father let his sister take me and raise me with her chillen. She was good to me, but befo' he let her have me he willed I must wear a bell till I was 21 year old, strapped 'round my shoulders with the bell 'bout three feet from my head in steel frame. That was for punishment for bein' born into the world a son of a white man and my mammy, a Negro slave. I wears this frame with the bell where I couldn't reach the clapper, day and night. I never knowed what it was to lay down in bed and get a good night's sleep till I was 'bout 17 year old, when my father died and my missy took the bell offen me.

"Befo' my father gave me to his sister, I was tied and strapped to a tree and whipped like a beast by my father, till I was unconscious, and then left strapped to a tree all night in cold and rainy weather. My father was very mean. He and he sister brung me to Texas, to North Zulch, when I 'bout 12 year old. He brung my mammy, too, and made her come and be his mistress one night every week. He would have kilt every one of his slaves rather than see us go free, 'specially me and my mammy.

"My missy was purty good to me, when my father wasn't right 'round. But he wouldn't let her give me anything to eat but cornbread and water and little sweat 'taters, and jus' 'nough of that to keep me alive. I was allus hongry. My mammy had a boy called Frank Adds and a girl called Marie Adds, what she give birth to by her cullud husban', but I never got to play with them. Missy worked me on the farm and there was 'bout 100 acres and fifteen slaves to work 'em. The overseer waked us 'bout three in the mornin' and then he worked us jus' long as we could see. If we didn't git 'round fast 'nough, he chain us to a tree at night with nothin' to eat, and nex' day. if we didn't go on the run he hit us 39 licks with a belt what was 'bout three foot long and four inches wide.

"I wore the bell night and day, and my father would chain me to a tree till I nearly died from the cold and bein' so hongry. My father didn't 'lieve in church and my missy 'lieved there a Lord, but I wouldn't have 'lieved her if she try larn me 'bout 'ligion, 'cause my father tell me I wasn't any more than a damn mule. I slep' on a chair and tried to res' till my father died, and then I sang all day, 'cause I knowed I wouldn't be treated so mean. When missy took that bell offen me I thinks I in Heaven 'cause I could lie down and go to sleep. When I did I couldn't wake up for a long time and when I did wake up I'd be scairt to death I'd see my father with his whip and that old bell. I'd jump out of bed and run till I give out, for fear he'd come back and git me.

"I was 'bout 17 year old then and I so happy not to have that bell on me. Missy make us work hard but she have plenty to eat and I could sleep. On Christmas she cook us a real dinner of beef meat.

"Plenty time I listens to the cannon popping till I mos' deaf, and I was messenger boy and spy on the blue bellies. When I'd git back to the Southern sojers I he'ped 'em bury they dead and some what was jus' wounded I he'ped carry home.

"When we heered was was over and we's free, we all jus' jumped up and hollers and dances. Missy, she cries and cries, and tells us we is free and she hopes we starve to death and she'd be glad, 'cause it ruin her to lose us. They was a big bunch of us niggers in town and we stirrin' 'round like bees workin' in and out a hive. We was jus' that way. I went wild and the first year I went north, but I come back 'gain to Texas.

"After 'while I marries a Indian maid. It was nothin' much but Indians 'round and there wasn't much law. I lived with her 'bout two year and then the Indians come and captured her jus' befo' she was to give birth. They kilt her or carried her 'way and lef' me for dead, and I never seed or heered of her since. While I was sick a outlaw, what was Tomas Jafferies, he'ped me git well and then I turns outlaw and follows all signs of Indians, all over the earth. But I never could git word of my wife.

"It mus' be 'bout 15 year after that, I marries Feline Ford, by a preacher. My first weddin' was common weddin' with the Indian maid. I jus' give her deerskin in front of Tomas Jefferies and she my wife."

ALLEN THOMAS

Allen Thomas, 97, was owned by several ranchers of Jefferson and Orange Counties, Texas, but recalls Moise Broussard of Hamshire the best. Ill health has affected his memory and his story is not coherent. He is a familiar figure on the streets of Beaumont, Texas, a small man clad in none too clean and somewhat ragged clothes, with a tow sack across his shoulders, into which he puts such things as he finds in his wanderings about the city. Rumor has it that Allen is fairly well to do and that his begging attitude is assumed, for reasons of his own.

"I figgers I's gwine be 97 year old on de fourth of August, I's borned over in Duncan Woods, over in Orange County. My daddy's name was Lockin Thomas. I never see my daddy. He git drown in de river here at Beaumont. My mammy's Hetty Anderson.

"I 'longed to three masters. One John Adam and he was mean. One Stowers, and he was mean but not so mean to me. Den dere Moise Broussard, he was purty mean, but he never beat me. De las' man what finish raise me was Amos Harrison and he purty good man. He wife name Mag and dey lives on Turtle Bayou over in Chambers County. He buy me from Lewis Pinder. He was good. My brudder was Kelly Idonia and I had a sister Lessie

Williams. Dey beat her with clubs. I's walk over many a dead person. Dey beat 'em to death.

"Us had tins dishes dem times, master and slaves, too. Dey have wooden paddles what us take de food out de dishes with. De white folks sot at one table and de cullud folks have table to deyself, but 'bout what de white folks has.

"Us have watermilion and sugar cane and milk and butter. Den us have de possum. Us clean him and put him top de house and 'low de frost fall on him. Den us fill him full salt and pepper and put him in de oven. Sometime put sweet 'taters all 'round him. Us have de long, square oven with de lid on it.

"Us wore knitted shirt make on dem looms and dey gives us boots with brass toes on 'em. Me and mammy work on de spinnin' wheel many a night up to one or two o'clock. I used to card de bats.

Allen Thomas

"Dere plenty hawgs and hosses and dem cattle what am longhorn. Us have plenty meat and raise veg'tables, too.

"I never seed no sojers but I heared de cannons. I

disremember when peace am corral'. I come up here to Beaumont when I thank I's a man and I's been here every Gawd's since.

"I see some sperrits, but I see 'em only special times. You see 'em twict a year, 'tween spring and summer and den 'gain 'twixt fall and winter. Sometime dey comes right 'long and den sometime dey jis' standin' still. When you looks at 'em dey looks kinder vagueish. I can allus tell when sperrits 'round. Dey got a queer scent. When you walk 'bout 20 feet, steam gwineter hit you in de face. I can tell dey dere iffen I can't see 'em. Dey look like men. Dey ain't white but dey got a pale look."

BILL AND ELLEN THOMAS

Bill and Ellen Thomas live in the Old Slave Settlement, 3 miles north of Hondo. Bill is 88 and Ellen is 81. They seem to be happy; their fields are tilled, a horse and a cow graze near the house; a kitchen garden is under way and several broods of baby chicks are in the yard. They were dressed in simple, clean clothes, and Ellen wears a string of nutmegs around her neck, to 'make yer eyes strong.'

Uncle Bill's Story

"Does you want me to start right at the beginnin'? Well, I'll tell you jes' how I went to this country. I left Falls County where I belonged to the man there that kept the post office. He was named Chamlin. He had lots of land, I reckin about 50 acres. They kep' us in a little house right in their yard. Reckin how old I was when he bought me? Jus' five years old! He give $500 for me, but he bought my mother and my sisters, too. He had to buy me, 'cause my mother, she wouldn't go without me. No, suh, she tol' 'em she wouldn't go if they didn' buy me, too. An' the man he bought us f'om, he wanted to keep me, so he wouldn't take less than $500 for me. Massa Chamblin bought the whole family, 'cept my father. They sold him and we never laid eyes on him again.

"My mother cooked. Massa Chamlin, he always fed us plenty, an' whatever they had, we had. If he cooked sausage, you had it too; if he cooked ham, you got it too; if he cooked lye hominy, you got it; an' if he had puddin', you got some.

"When I was 6 or 7 years old I chopped cotton and I plowed too, and I could lay as straight rows with oxen as any you ever saw.

"The massa whipped me with a dogwood switch, but he never did bring no blood. But it taken 7 men to whip my father.

"I'll tell you how I got away f'om there. Massa bought cotton and carried it to Mexico. He taken his 2 boys with him and we had 3 wagons and I drove one. I had 4 oxen and I had 3 bales of cotton on my wagon; he had 6 oxen and 6 bales of cotton, and the last wagon, it had 10 bales on it and 6 oxen. He had to ship it acrost the Rio Grande. If a Mexican bought it, he come across and took it over hisself. Reckin how much he got for that cotton? He got 60¢ a pound. Yes'm, he sho' did. Cotton was bringin' that then.

"I was freed over there in Mexico. I was about 14 years old. Massa Chamlin, he stayed over there till the country was free. He didn't believe in that fightin'.

"I cooked in a hotel over there in Mexico. I cooked two years at $1.00 a day.

"When Massa owned me, he always give us good clothes. Our pants was made out of duckin' like wagon sheets, but my mother took some kind of bark and dyed 'em. I think it was blackjack bark. He give us shoes, too. They was half-tan leather brogans."

"I used to play the fiddle for dances when I was young, but not after I joined the church. I played for the white people. Oh, yes'm, the cullud folks had dances, they sho' did dance.

"Yes'm, I saw a ghost onct. One night after I was livin' down here, I was goin' to Sabinal, me and another man, and a great long thing passed right in front of us. It was the blackest thing you ever saw. It was about six feet long. Yes'm, it sho' was a ghost or sumpin; it disappeared, and me lookin' at it. The other fellow that was with me, he seen it, too.

"Yes, they was lots of panthers and bears here. If this ghost was a bear, he sho' was a big 'un. We had a ghost down here on the creek we called the 'Ball Water Hole Ghost.' He was seen lots of times. He used to stay down there, but he ain't been seen lately. My wife, she seen him."

Aunt Ellen's Story

"Yes'm, I seen him walkin' 'long the trail ahead of us. He had on a black hat, like a tall stovepipe hat, and a long black coat, and when we got up close he jes' disappeared. He was a big man, and tall, too. We didn' know which way he went; he jes' seemed to disappear. My oldest daughter saw him too. Lots of folks did. He was always seen down at that water hole somewhere.

"Another time, I was stayin' with Mrs. Reedes. Mr. Reedes was killed and all night long he'd come back and grind coffee and sprinkle it all over us. I was so bad scared I nearly died. Next mornin' there'd be coffee all over the floor. We supposed it was Mr. Reede's ghost. They say if a person was wicked they come back like that. Onct he pulled Mrs. Reedes outta bed and pitched her on the floor, and he would take the dishes out of the shelves and throw 'em down. I couldn't stand it but a night or two and I said I was goin' home. Yes, ma'am, it sho' was a ghost. He sho' did tear up that house every night. Why, they'd be a light shine in that room just as plain as daylight, nearly. They say ghosties will run you, but I never had any to run me."

"I was born in Mississippi. We come to Texas and my mother died, so grandma raised me. I was jes' a baby when we come to Texas. Mr. Harper owned us. I remember the war, but it's so long ago I don't remember much. I remember when John Harper read the free paper to us. He had a big lot of slaves, but

when he read, the free papers they jes' flew out like birds. But I didn't. I was stickin' to my grandmother. She was on crutches and she stayed on at the Harper place.

Bill and Ellen Thomas

"After we was free I worked for them a long time. I cooked, washed, ironed, milked the cows. He was pretty good to us, Judge Harper was. I went along with him when he went to war, his wife and chillun did too, and I nursed them, I'd give a young baby shuck tea to break him out with the hives. For chills and fever I give quinine weed. It don't grow here.

"When Judge Harper went up to Hondo my grandma grabbed me and kept me. So I stayed and worked. I was still a young girl, but I plowed, hauled and grubbed. I used to wear 'cotton stripes.' I remember 'em well. It was a homespun cloth. I know how to spin and weave and I could knit a pair of socks in two nights.

"I never did hear much about hard times. I was treated good but I got switched many a time. Oh, yes'm. I've been whipped, but not like some of 'em was. They used to tie some of 'em down. I've heered tell, they shore whopped 'em. They used to be a runaway that got away and went to Mexico now and then, and if they caught him they shore whopped him awful.

"That old piano in there, my daughter bought a long time ago. The varnish is off, but a man tol' us it could be sandpapered and refinished and it would be a beautiful thing. It's about 75 years old."

LUCY THOMAS

Lucy Thomas, 86, was born in Harrison Co., Texas, a slave of Dr. William Baldwin. She stayed with her master until 1868. In 1869 she married Anthony Thomas. She now lives with her son at Baldwin Switch, sixteen miles northeast of Marshall, Texas, on part of the land originally owned by the Baldwins.

"My name am Lucy Baldwin Thomas and I's birthed right here in Harrison County, on the old Baldwin place at Fern Lake. The log cabin where I's birthed sot in a grove of trees right by the lake. The Baldwin place jined the Haggerty and Major Andrews places.

"The best statement I can make of my age am I's 'bout fourteen the last year of Abe Lincoln's war. It was true, 'cause I starts hoein' in the field when I's nine years old and I'd been hoein' a long time.

"They called my papa, Ike. The Baldwins bought him out of Alabama, and mama's name was Nancy and she's birthed in Virginny, and the Baldwins bought her out the New Orleans slave market for $1,100.00. I's heared my gran'ma, Barbara, tell how some Alabama owners drug they niggers with a mule and laid dem face down in a hole and beat dem till they's raw as beefsteak. But her folks wasn't like that and the Baldwins wasn't neither. They was good white folks, and Missy was named May Amelia and then there was Old Marse Doctor William. He was a doctor but he worked a hundred acres land and owned 'bout eighty-five niggers, what lived in log quarters. They had son-of-a-gun beds peg to the walls, and wore bachelor brogan shoes and blue and stripe lowel clothes made on the place, and had lots to eat. My mama say she had a lots better time in slavery than after.

"All hands was up and in the field by daylight and Marse Baldwin allus kep' a fifty gallon barrel whiskey on the place and a demijohn on the front porch all the time for the niggers to git they drink on way to the field. But nobody ever got drunk.

"Marse's brother-in-law, Marse Lewis Brantly, was overseer, but never kicked and beat the niggers. He give us a light breshin' when we needed it. We would go mos' anywhere but had to git a pass first, and had play parties on Saturday night.

Lucy Thomas

"I went to school three months. A Yankee named Old Man Mills run a school and I quit workin' in the field to go. Them days, the Klu Kluxers was runnin' round and I seed big bunches of niggers with they heads tied up, goin' to report the Kluxers to the Progee Marshal.

"Three years after it was all over, my folks moved to the Haggerty place. I know lots 'bout old Col. Haggerty's widow. She was an Indian and her first husband was a big chief of the Caddo Indians on Caddo Lake. He betrayed the Indians to the white folks and he and her hid on a cave on the lake, and she slipped out to git food, and the Indians took him away. They say they scalped him like they done white folks. Then she married Col. Haggerty and he got kilt on a gamblin' spree and left her a lot of land and 'bout three hundred slaves. She kept a nigger woman chained to a loom for a year and when she knew the slaves was gittin' free, she poisoned a lot of dem and buried dem at night. We'd hear the other slaves moanin' and cryin' at night for the dead ones. That widow Haggerty was somthin'!

"I seed the 'Mattie Stephens' boat the day after it burned and kilt sixty people. Me and Anthony Thomas went to Marshall and married the day 'fore it burnt. That was on February 12th, in 1869. I lived with him fifty-five years and raised seven chillen, and after he died I kep' on farmin' until 'bout three years ago. Then I come to live with one my son's here and this land we're on right now was part the land old Marse Baldwin owned. I gits $10.00 a month from the gov'ment. They sho' is good to me, and my son is good, too, so I's happy in my old age."

PHILLES THOMAS

Philles Thomas, 77, was born a slave of Dave Miles, who owned a plantation in Brazoria Co., Texas. Philles does not remember her father, but was told by her mother that he was sent to the Confederate Army and was fatally injured at Galveston, Texas. Philles stayed with her family until she was seventeen, then married William Thomas. They now live at 514 Hayes St., Fort Worth, Tex.

"I don't 'member much 'bout de war, 'cause I's jus' a young'un when it start and too small to have much mem'randum when it stop. I's still on de place where I's born when surrender come, de Lowoods Place, own by Massa Dave Miles, 'twixt Brazoria and Columbia. Massa Dave sho' have de big plantation but I don' know how many slaves.

"When I's a young'un, us kids didn't run round late. We'uns am put to bed. When sundown come, my mammy see dat my feets am wash and de gown put on, and in de bunk I goes.

"I can't 'member my daddy, but mammy told me him am sent to de 'Federate Army and am kilt in Galveston. She say dey puttin' up breastworks and de Yanks am shootin' from de ships. Well, daddy am watchin' de balls comin' from dem guns, fallin' round dere, and a car come down de track loaded with rocks and hit him. Dat car kilt him.

"Mammy marries Bill Bailey after freedom and moves to de Barnum Place, what Massa John Miles own. I stays with mammy till I's seventeen and holp dem share crop. Den I leaves. Dat de way with chillen, dey gives you lots of trouble raisin' dem and den off dey goes. When my chillen am young'uns dey's on my lap, and when dey's growed up, dey's on my heart.

"Us have de hard time share croppin'. Times was hard den and de niggers didn't know much 'bout takin' care demselves. Course, dey better off free, but dey have to larn. Us work hard and make 'nough to live on de first year us free. Us raise cotton and veg'tables and when I's not helpin' mammy I goes out and gits a li'l work here and yonder.

"I marries in Galveston, to dat old cuss, settin' right dere, William Thomas am he name and I's stood for him ever since. Him am dock wallopin' when I's marry to him. Sho', him am a dock walloper. If you wants to talk big, you calls it stev'dore on de wharf.

"Dat cullud gen'man of mine allus brung in de bacon. We'uns am never rich, but allus eats till de last few years. Us goes on de farm and it hand and mouth livin', but us eats someway. After while, us come to Fort Worth and he works as mortar man and cement mixer. We'uns live good till de few years back, when him break down in de back and can't work no more.

"It am ten chillun us raise but only five livin' now. One live at Stop Six, right here in Fort Worth, and de others am all over de world. Us don't know where dey am. Since Bill can't work no more, us git de pension from de State and dat $26.00 de month for de two of us.

"Does I ever vote? Christ for 'mighty! No. Why yous talk dat foolishment. Why for dis igno'mous old woman want to vote? No, sar, and no tother womens ought to vote. Dat am for de mens to do. My Bill votes couple times, when us in Galveston, and I tells you 'bout dat.

"Dey gives de eddication with a couple cups whiskey and de cheroot. When de whiskey and de cheroot works on Bill's brain, dere am den de smart nigger, and he votes 'telligent. I asks him what he votes for and him say, 'I's vote for what am on de ticket.' 'What am on de ticket,' I says. 'How does I know, I can't read.' Den I says, 'Better yous not vote, 'cause maybe yous vote to put youself in de jailhouse.' So I guess him think 'bout dat and him see what foolishment and troublement him maybe git into, and him quit votin'. We'uns am lucky with de trouble. Guess it 'cause we'uns knows how to 'have. When I's young my mammy larn me how to 'have and where I 'long, so de patterrollers and de Ku Klux never bother we'uns. Now, we'uns so old us can't git round, so us double safe now.

Philles Thomas

"Gosh for 'mighty! What yous want next? Now it for me to sing. Well, yous can't put de bluff on dis old nigger, so here it am:

"'Put on my long white robe,

>   Put on de golden crown,
>   Put on de golden slipper,
>   And forever be Jesus' lamb.'

"But I likes 'nother song better, like dis:

>   "'Herodias go down to de river one day,
>   Want to know what John Baptist have to say,
>   John spoke de words at risk of he life,
>   Not lawful to marry yous brudder's wife.'

"Not dat am 'nough. If I's here much longer, yous have dis old woman dancin'."

WILLIAM M. THOMAS

William M. Thomas, 87, now residing at 514 Hayes St., Fort Worth, Texas, was born a slave of Dr. Frank Thomas, in Lauderdale County, Miss. William's father was sold when William was a baby and his mother mated with another slave. It was seven years after they were freed that the family left their master and moved onto a tract of land. William stayed with them until he was twenty-four, then worked twelve years in Galveston, as a stevedore. He farmed until 1910, then worked as a mortar man at the Purina Mills in Fort Worth until 1931. He and his wife receive a $13.00 monthly pension.

"I knows 'zactly how old I is. Massa done give my mammy de statement. He do dat for all he niggers when dey freed. I's borned May 17th, in 1850, and dat make me eighty-eight next May. Dat's on Massa Doctor Frank Thomas's plantation, over near Meridian, in Mississippi. Dere forty-four slave families on he place and he own 'bout seven hunerd acres land, so him have plenty pasture, wood and field land. De money crop was cotton, of course.

"My mammy and sis was in de place and my steppa. My pappy am sold and took to Texas when I's so li'l I don't 'member him. After dat, mammy done took another man.

"All de slaves live in quarters 'cept de house servants, and dey live in servants' quarters, and dere's where I's de lucky nigger. My mammy am cook for massa and I's round de kitchen what 'twas plenty of good eats. And I plays with massa's two boys, 'twas Frank and Lawrence.

"I's so li'l 'fore surrender I never really works, 'cept to be de errand boy. I fetches eggs and sich. Massa have lots of chickens and us fetch in high as a thousand eggs in one day sometimes. Us have eggs to eat, too. Massa Thamas am awful good and dere am never de holler 'bout feedin'. I bet none dem niggers done live so good after dey free.

"Us have all de meat us want, mostest pork and beef and mutton. Dey kills five hunderd hawgs when killin' time came, and make hams and bacon and sausages. If yous ever ate sich ham and bacon what am made by massa's butcher right dere on de place, you say dere never am sich. Dat sausage, it make de mouf water to think 'bout it. 'Sides de meat, us have cornbread and 'lasses and de rations ain't measure out, 'cept de white flour on Sunday mornin'. All week de meals am cook in dat kitchen and serve in de big shed, but each family cook for deyself on Sunday.

"Us go to church if us want, 'bout four miles off. Massa give anybody de pass to go dere. Dere am no parties and sich, but old Jack saw on de fiddle and us sing.

"Massa didn't whip, only once. Dat 'cause a nigger steal he fav'rite pumpkin. He am savin' dat for to git de seed and it am big as de ten gallon jug. De corn field am full of pumpkins, but dat nigger done took massa's choice one. Dat pumpkin am so big, he have to tussle with it 'fore he git it to he cabin. It like stealin' a elephant, you can't hide it in de watch pocket. Course, lots of niggers seed dat cullud gen'man with dat pumpkin, and 'fore long massa knew it.

"Well, sar, it am de funny sight to see him punish dat nigger. First, massa set him down on de ground front de quarters, where us all see him. Den he make dat nigger set down and give him de big bowl pumpkin sauce and make him eat it. Him eat and eat and git so full him can't hardly swallow and massa say, 'Eat some more, it am awful good.' Dat nigger try, but him can't eat no more. Massa give him de light breshin' and it am funny to see, dat cullud gen'man with pumpkin smear on he face and tears runnin' down he face. After dat, us chillen call him Massa Pumpkin and massa never have no more trouble with stealin' he seed pumpkins.

"When war starts I's 'bout fifteen year old. 'Bout half mile from de plantation am de crossroads and one go to New Orleans and one go to Vicksburg. Dere am a 'Federate camp dere at de start, but after 'while dey goes and de Yanks comes. Dere a battle near, and us hear de shootin' but us have to stay on de place.

"I done slip off and see de camp, though. De Yanks puts up two big tents and use dem for de hospital and de wounded am fetch dere. What I sees and hears dere, I never forgits, and it done turn dis nigger 'gainst war. Why can't dey settle dey 'sputes without killin'? Dey's moanin' and cryin' and screamin' in dem tents.

"One day de Yanks come clean de crib of all de corn and de meat house of all de meat. Massa am smart and fix it so dey don't find all de rations. Him dig a big ditch in de woods and hide lots of rations.

"Us didn't know when freedom came. It a long time after dat de Yanks come tell us, and it de same way on all de plantations round dere. De Yanks come and make massa pay us all fifty cents de day. After dat massa puts dem what wants to go on pieces of land and dey ain't charge for it till seven year after. Den dey has to pay rent and part de crop, and for de mules and tools all de time.

"I stays with my folks till I's twenty-four year old and den I's on my way to Galveston and gits work as de stevedore. Dat am on de wharf and I works dere twelve year. I votes dere two times. Some white folks done come to us, and de boss, too, and gives us de ticket. It am all mark up. Boss say us don't have to work de next day, and us to report at a place. When us comes dere, 'twas a table with meat and bread and stuff for to eat, and whiskey and cigars. Dey give us something to eat and a cup or two of dat whiskey and puts de cigar in de mouth. Us am 'portant niggers, ready to vote. With dat cup of whiskey in de stomack and dat cigar in de mouth and de hat cock on side de head, us march to de votin' place and does our duty. Fix up de way us was, us would vote to put us back in slavery. And de nigger what didn't vote, after all dat, him am in for de fixin'. I means he gits fixed. Dey pounds he head till him won't forgit to do it right next time.

"But I gits to thinkin' how massa say when us leave him, 'Don't let no white folks use you for to make trouble.' I figgers dat what am happenin' with dat votin' business, and I quits votin' and goes to farmin'. I 'lieve de cullud folks should vote, but not de igno'mous niggers like us was den.

William M. Thomas

I farms till 1910 and den comes to Fort Worth, and dey am buildin' de Purina Mills Elevators on East 4th Street and I works dere at mortar work. Den I works at cement on lots de big buildin's in dis city, till 'bout ten year ago, when it git too hard for me. I has de back misery.

"I gits married to Phillis Wilson when I's twenty-nine, in Galveston, and us don't allushave lots, but us gits by and raises de family. Now us have to live on de pension from de State, what am $13.00, and sometimes us am awful short, tryin' to pay de rent and buy de rations and what clothes us needs, but us am glad to git it. Ten chillen am what us raises and five am dead and four am scattered and us don't know where, and one live here.

""Ain't it diff'rent how peoples lives? Us used to travel with de ox and now dey flies in de sky. Folks sings in New York and us sets right here and hears dem. Shucks! De way things am gwine, I's all fussed up and can't understand whether I's gwine or comin'."

MARY THOMPSON

Mary Thompson was born a slave 87 years ago, in Denton, Miringo County, Alabama. Her mother, Viney Askew, and father, Wesley Jones, belonged to Green Askew, a Georgian. She was 15 when she was freed. Mary now lives at 1104 East Avenue, Austin, Tex.

"I was bo'n in Alabama and my mother was Viney Askew. She belonged to Marster Green Askew. My father was Wesley Jones, 'cause he took his marster's name.

"My mother was a good cook and she cooked for de marster. She had a great big stove and she made salt-risin' bread, too. We and all de slaves lived in cabins near de big house and some of de slaves would have chillen by de marster.

"When we come home from de fields at night, de women cooked de food and den dey was so tired dey jus' went to bed. We didn' have fun in de evenin's, but on Christmas mornin' de marster give us eggnog and sich. Den we'd sing but I don' 'member de songs now.

"De crops in Alabama would be cleared by July 4 and den we'd have sev'ral days off, all de slaves. Dey'd give us pits of barbecue and pies and cakes to eat.

"When we was sick de marster would sen' for de doctor and we made teas outta herbs and sich. Alabama was full of chills and fevers in dem days and we drunk catnip tea for fevers and blue and white sage. Calamus root, looks like an onion, was good for de chillens' colic.

"My mistress' niece had a big plantation and she had a place whar she had de slaves whopped. She had a reg'lar whoppin' post. My marster jes' had a large cowhide whoop. Yes, I got a whoppin' more'n once. Sev'ral times marster took hold my ears and bumped my head 'gainst de wall. But gen'rally dey was good to me.

"We wasn't 'lowed no whiskey, 'less we was sick. De poor white folks was good to us, better'n rich folks. Dey'd give us a quarter now'n den.

"I can 'member how de slaves was fattened like hawgs and den marched to town and 'round and auctioned off like cattle. Some of 'em had done somethin' mean and was sold off. Some of 'em brought more'n a thousand dollars down in New Orleans.

"I knows of one slave who liked to run 'round at night. She was nuss to marster's girl and she give it morphine to put it to sleep. She give de baby girl so much morphine dat her body was full of it and she died. De cullud folks got to talkin' too much and de baby was dug up and 'xamined. De slave nuss was put in jail and kep' there a long time and den she was sold.

"Heap of de slaves would run away and go up north. Dey would try to find 'em by sendin' nigger houn's after 'em. Once de houn's caught a slave and he kep' sayin', 'O, Lawd ... O, Lawd!'

Mary Thompson

"After de war, when we was free, de slaves would go here and there and a lot of 'em died. Dey'd git de black measles, go out in de woods and die. Dey didn' know how to take care of demselves.

"I stayed at marster's house eight months, den hired out at ten dollars a month. Dat was de fus' money I ever made and I didn' want to go to school, 'cause I wanted to make dat money. Dat looked like big money to me. I was proud to have it, 'cause I could git what I wanted. I cain't read or write to this day.

"I was married to General Thompson, and he'd been a slave too, in Alabama. Yes, General was his given name. I was 16 years old when I married and a white preacher married us durin' a 4th of July celebration. Yes, we had a big time and a good time.

"We come to Texas later and my husban' farmed on the Brazos. We had eight chillen, and two of 'em is livin.' My husban' died and I buried him, den I took up with a Horace Foster, and he was nothin' but a gambler. I lived with him 'bout 8 years, but he never would marry me, so I lef' him."

PENNY THOMPSON

Penny Thompson, 86, now living at 1100 E. 12th St., Fort Worth, Texas, was born a slave to Calvin Ingram, in Coosa Co., Alabama. In 1867 Penny was brought to Tyler, Texas, and several years later she married Ike Thompson and moved to Fort Worth.

"Do I 'member slavery days? Yes, suh! How could I forget dem? For an old person I has good 'collection. I's 10 year old when de war start and my massa am Calvin Ingram. My mammy and pappy was a weddin' present to Massa Ingram from his pappy. Mammy give birth to 15 chilluns, but I never saw any of my brothers and sisters, 'cause they all born on Massa Ingram's pappy's plantation 'fore he give my mammy to Massa Ingram.

"De plantation dat Massa Ingram have was 200 acres or mo'. Him own 'bout 20 grown-up slaves, and on dat place dey raises 'bout everything we eats and wears, includin' de vinegar and de peach brandy. Everybody am 'signed to dey duties and my mammy am chief cook for de big house. I he'ps her and feeds chickens, gits eggs and totes water.

"De treatmen' couldn't be better. Massa am de bestes' and de kindes' fellow dat ever live. He am in Heaven, for sho', but de missy mus' be in Hell, for she sho' was a debbil. Massa have de fight with her lots of times 'bout de treatment of us, but he wouldn't let her 'buse us.

"We'uns was never hongry for food, 'cause we have lots of meat, chickens and eggs and cornmeal and 'lasses and honey. De hams is smoked on de place and dey am de hams, white man, dey am de hams! Den massa have a big cellar jus' full of everything and I never forgit de big, brass key what lock dat cellar. Dere was de jams and de jellies and de preserves, and de massa give us somethin' of all of dat. Him makes de gran' peach brandy and every mornin' we could have two fingers in de glass. 'Twas de same at night. Dere was somethin' else was reg'lar every mornin' and night and dat am de prayer. He calls all us together and says de prayers. I often thinks of dat brandy and de prayers, two times every day.

"As for de whuppin,' dere wasn't any on massa's place. Him have only one nigger what am unruly and dat am Bill McClure, and a bigger thief never lived.

"On de nex' plantation dey gives de whuppin' and we hears dem niggers beller. On dat plantation dey trades and sells de niggers all de time and de speculation wagon comes by often. Sometime it am awful to see de babies sold from de mothers and de wife from de husban'. Sich bemoanin' at some of dem sales, yous jus' can't 'magine.

"But on massa's place we has no tradin' of slaves and we'uns have pass for go to church and parties and de dance. When de night for de party come on our place, de yard am cleaned off and we makes sandwiches. One time massa come to me and say, 'Jus' wait a minute, I nearly forgits de mos' 'portant part,' and he give me a new pink dress. I's so happy I cries for joy, and everybody says I looks like de Queen of Sheba.

"De other big time am de corn huskin' bee. Once a year all de neighbors comes fust to one place den to de other. At de huskin's, dey gives de prize when you finds a red ear. De prize am two fingers of dat peach brandy. When dey gits de fus' one dey works a little harder, de second still faster, and de third, Lawd-a-massy, how dem husks do fly! Dey don't git drunk, 'cause you am lucky to find as much as three red ears at one huskin'.

"We has de weddin's too, but no preacher or cer'mony. When a man sees a girl him likes and de girl am willin', dey says dey wants a weddin'. De womens cooks extra and dey gits de cedar boughs and wets dem and sprinkles flour on dem and puts dem on de table. We sits at de table and eats and sings 'ligious songs and after supper dey puts de broom on de floor an de couple takes de hands and steps over de broom, and den dey am put to bed.

Penny Thompson

"We was never bother with de patter rollers, but I 'members a song 'bout dem, like dis:

"'Up de hill and down de hollow
Patter rollers cotched nigger by de collar;

Dat nigger run, dat nigger flew,
Dat nigger tear his shirt in two.'

"In de war soldiers comes to massa's place and every time he feeds dem. You hears de clippity clop of de hosses and dey is off de saddle 'fore you gits to de door. Dey says, 'We wants de meal,' or maybe dey wants to sleep. Massa's wife say, 'I's not goin' do nothin' for dem blue bellies,' but massa make her fix de chicken. Dere was everything dere but manners, 'cause dey have de pistols drawed.

"After freedom, mos' of us stays with massa, 'cause we don't know where to go and we don't want to go, but 'fore long massa dies and dat was mournin' time. After de death, we all leaves.

I marries Bill Thompson but he won't work so after 15 year I gits de divorcement."

ALBERT TODD

Albert Todd, 86 years old, was born a slave to Capt. Hudson, in Russellville, Kentucky. His master was killed in the Civil War and he then came to Texas in a covered wagon. His "Missus" kept him a slave for three years after the War. He now lives with his wife, daughter and two sons at 703 Center St., San Antonio, Texas.

"I most suppose my memory is too jumpy, but I'll try to bring it 'long from de time I was born. I don't know de year, but it was in Russellville, Kentucky and my massa, Captain Hudson, had a fruit orchard. My reg'lar work was protectin' my young missus, Nannie Hudson. She had to walk five miles to and forth from school every day and I was her protector. I was only 8 and she was 11. I sat on the steps until she got through larnin' and then brung her home. She come to be grown and married and died, but I allus loved her.

"When war comes, my massa goes and gets kilt and my missus got 'gusted with the orchard and packs up in two covered wagons and heads crossland to Texas. We finally gets to Lavernia and gets a farm and us worked plenty hard.

Albert Todd

"Our missus was good to us, but one white man neighbor got a new set of niggers every year. He say if they didn't die, they wasn't any good work left in them after they works for him a year. He allus cut off one they ears, so if they run away he'd know 'em.

"My clothes was a long shirt, made out of a meal sack. That's all I wore them days. I was a slave three year after the others was freed, 'cause I didn't know nothin' 'bout bein' free. A Mrs. Gibbs got holt of me and makes me her slave. She was a cruel old woman and she didn't have no mercy on me. She give me one sausage and one biscuit in the mornin' and nothin' else all day. One day she gone and I stole some biscuits, and she comes back and says, 'Did you take them biscuits?' She tells me if I tells de truth she won't punish me, but she knocks me down and beats me till I not know nothin'. But after 'while her house burns and she burns up in it.

"But 'fore that I was goin' to run away and I goes to the road and sits down and then my sisters comes 'long and finds me and takes me to a place where they was livin' on the ranch of a man name Widman. We works for him a long time and then I is free from that Gibbs woman."

ALECK TRIMBLE

H is skin was of an extremely dark chocolate color, his hair thin and gray. A blue shirt was about his body while blue trousers enclosed his nether limbs. His bare feet protruded as he sat on an old dilapidated chair. Under his flat nose was a gray mustache, and one eye had completely lost its vision. This small negro man was Aleck Trimble who thoughtfully told the story of his life. [HW: Veth, Tex.]

"I was bo'n in 1861. I warn't much of a chile when freedom come, but yet dey's right smart of t'ings I kin 'member in slavery times."

"My pa name was Aleck Trimble and dat's my name, too. My ma was Ellen Trimble and I was de onlies' son. I didn' hab no brudders. Ol' marster's las' name was Alexander, but I dis'member his fus' name."

"I uster hafter do a li'l wuk 'roun' de place like pullin' up weeds and drivin' de calfs. I 'member one time I was drivin' a calf up to de lot and I saw a crazy man. He didn' try to do nuffin' to me. I jis' walk up on him and he sittin' dere mumblin' and I know right den dere was sump'n' wrong wid him. He didn' try to hu't me nor run atter me, but he sho' scare me and I run away from him fas' as I kin."

"I warn't so glad when freedom come. I was a-farin'

pretty well in de kitchen. I didn' t'ink 'eber see better times dan what dem was, and I ain't. I t'ought I was jis' as near hebben as I want to be. It didn' look to me like dey coulder been no betterer dan what dey was."

"I uster had jis' all I want to eat. Us hab biscuit and syrup, and plenty milk and butter. And dey give us all de collard greens and hog jowls us could hol'."

"Dey uster had lots of cows and all de milk and butter anybody want. Dey had a big bucket hangin' in de well. Dey put de butter in dat in de summer time to keep it from meltin'. How dey kep' it from sp'ilin'? Why, dey et it up, dat's how dey keep it from sp'ile."

"I neber see 'em do de slaves bad. Iffen dey did dey tek 'em off in de woods somers where nobody see 'em."

"Sometime nigger traders come 'long de road wid a big drove of niggers. I neber pay dat no min' though. It was jis' a drove of niggers to me."

"Dey gimme 'bout as good clo's as I got now. When I was doin' 'roun' de yard at Marster' house I wo' a shu't wid pleats 'cross de bosom in front."

"Dey gimme some britches befo' freedom come, and den I t'ought I's 'bout as big as anybody. Dey gimme dem when I was big 'nuff to dribe de calfs up from de lot. But I neber go in de fiel' to wuk."

"Atter freedom come I go to school to a white lady name' Mrs. Tunsten she had a son name' Waddy. She teach de school at Shiloh and all de white chillun and nigger chillun go to school in de same room. She teach her own chillun in dat school on de Huntsville road. I 'member de stages and t'ings gwine by. I t'ought she was a good teacher, but she whip me half a day one time 'cause I didn' spell "gangrene." She whip me 'till I learn how to spell it and I ain't neber forgit. I kin spell dat word yit. I's satisfy she from de Nor'f. Dere was a ol' stage stan' dere by de school house."

"I went to dat teacher and dat school t'ree or fo' year'. Atter she quit teachin' dey was other teachers what come drappin' in and teachin' t'ree or fo' months."

"My pa he uster wuk in de fiel' 'till freedom come. My ma she wuk in de kitchen. Dat how come I git so much outer de kitchen to eat. Sometime she hafter wuk in de fiel' too."

"Jis' like I say, I stay 'roun' de big house. I raise up wid de white chillun 'till I was 25 or 30 year' ol'."

"I t'ink dey stay at de ol' place a year or mo' atter freedom. Den dey 'gin to drif' 'roun' to diff'rent place w'ere dey find wuk to do. I stay wid de ol' folks and he'p s'po't (support) 'em wid what money I git for de wuk what I doin'. My ma lef' my pa at de ol' plantation, and her and me and a gal what was ol'er dan me, what was my sister, us move."

"De fus' wuk I done and de fus' money I mek was pickin' cotton for a white man. De fus' money I git I buy me a ol' Webster Blue-back speller. Lawd, I uster look at dat book sometime 'till dem A B C's all run togedder seem like."

"Dat plantation was de Johnnie Murchison plantation. Us stay dere 'bout five or six year'. Atter dat I lef' dere and went to wuk for cullud man what was name'

Sam Scott. I wuk 'roun' in de fiel' and go to mill when I was on dat place."

"I 'member seein' de sojers. Dey was a big troop of 'em come marchin' down de road. Dey was all of 'em dress' up in blue coats and some of 'em had blue capes over dey shoulders. Dey had wagons and lots of sich t'ings comin' 'long behin'."

"I can't tell you much 'bout de ol' marster 'cause I didn' see him eb'ry day. Lots and lots of time I didn' hab no notion where he was."

"Dey was a large troop of cullud folks on de place. When dey want 'em dey blow a bugle or ho'n or sump'n'."

"I git marry in Houston county. I don' 'member what year it was but it was back in Cleveland's 'ministration. Den atter while she die and dat lef' me a widower. Den 'bout 28 year' ago I marry Ollie Washington. I was wukkin' for Scott befo' I marry Washington. Dat's my li'l 'dopted gran'chile dere. You see dat t'ing 'roun' her neck? Dat's hoss hair roll up in a clo'f. Dat to he'p when she teethin'. Dat good for stomach and bowel trouble, too. Long as she wear dat she ain't gwine to hab no fever in de head needer. I gwine to let her wear it 'till she finish cuttin' her teef. I jis' put dat rag 'roun' it to keep it from stickin' her. You kin see how healthy she is."

"Anudder t'ing what good for chillun when dey's teethin' is for to tek a rabbit head and 'noint (anoint) dey gums good wid rabbit brains. Some of de ol' folks wear a dime tie' 'roun' dey leg wid a hole in it for de rheumatism."

"May-apple for a good purgative too, but you got to

know how to use it. Iffen you don' use it right though, it gwine to stir up your stomach and mek you sick. And you better not drink no milk when you tek dat May-apple root and you don' want to eat nuffin' needer. Dat's bitter'n quinine."

"Co'se, sometime some of de slaves die on de plantation. I know dey have home-mek coffin, but I ain't neber see 'em mekin' one. Sometime' when de corpse a-layin' dere dead dey have a wake."

"Dem what wanted 'em had a li'l patch of groun' where dey plant garden truck and veg'tables for deyself. Dey have half a day off on Sunday, and den co'se, dey have Sunday. All de slaves have big holiday on Crismus."

"Dey lib in log houses. Moss and du't (dirt) was pack' all in 'tween de logs and boards was nail' on over dat. Ol' marster he have a awful large house buil' outer plank. It had a gallery to de front and back."

"Dey had a li'l house down de way dey had preachin' in. De white preacher he do de preachin'. Seem to me dat soon play out."

"Dey had a ol' lady what ten' to de chillun when dey in de fiel' pickin' cotton. Sometime she uster sing:

> 'My Lord say dey's room enough,
> Room enough in hebben fer us all.'

fotch (fetch) 'em a whack on de head and say:

> 'Come 'long wid dat row.'"

"Atter freedom come de darkies uster have a song what go like dis:

> 'Come along

Come along
Make no delayin'
Soon be so Uncle Sam give us
all a farm.
'Come from de way
Come from de nation
'Twon't be long 'till Uncle Sam
give us all a farm.'

Atter while de Klu Kluxers git atter de cullud folks. Den dey mek a song:

'Run nigger run de Klu Klux git you.'

Lots of time dey come on Sunday. One place dere was a big plum thicket 'long de road and dey dodge in dere and ketch people. Lots of cullud folks hafter pass by dere to git where dey gwine. In de day time dem Klu Kluxes was jis' in dey common clo's but when dey come in de nights dey did figger deyself wid dem high p'int hats and white t'ings wrap 'roun' 'em."

"I b'longs to de Baptis' Chu'ch. I reckon dat was de Baptis' chu'ch back in dem days, but I don' 'member no baptisms back in slavery. I 'members though that dey was a blin' cullud man what uster preach."

"I 'members dey was lots of smallpox one time. Dat was atter freedom come, 'bout 50 year' ago. De people was sho' scare' of it, wusser'n if it was a Winchester. When I fus' 'member 'bout dat smallpox dey was a man had it and dey run him 'bout a mont' and bu'n him. If dey find out you got de smallpox you jis' long gone, you better not go out nor in. Dey put de food on de gate-pos'. If you don' git better in so many days dey bu'n you and de house and eb'ryt'ing up."

"I uster farm 'till de boll weevil start in dis part of de country. Atter dat sawmillin' and public works. Jis' go from one sawmill to anudder. But I spen' my bes' days on de farm."

"When I was cut off dem sawmill and public works jobs I was done wo' out. Dey orter stop' me fifteen years befo' dey did, 'cause den I mightenter (might not have) been wo' out. Now I can't do nuffin'."

"I los' one of my eye 'bout seben year' ago. I have de fever and it settle in my eye and jis' cook. Dat was when I had meningitis."

"I can't plow no mo'. I jis' live on my li'l bit of pension and dat ain't nuttin'."

REEVES TUCKER

Reeves Tucker, 98 year old Negro farmer of Harrison Co., Texas, was born in Bibb Co., Alabama, a slave of George Washington Tucker, Sr. When Reeves was six his master died and Reeves was separated from his family and brought to Texas by George Tucker, Jr. Reeves now lives with his son, who owns a farm nine miles northwest of Marshall, Texas.

"My father was Armistead Tucker and my mother Winnie Tucker and they's both born slaves of Massa George Washington Tucker. He lived over in old Alabama, between Selma and Maplesville. My brothers was Andy and John and Peter and there was two girls, Anne and Dorcus, and we was all born on Massa Tucker's plantation. My missy died 'fore I was born and my old massa died when I was jest a shirt-tail boy and his chillen had a dividement of his lands and mammy and all the chillen but me fell to the daughter and pappy was give to the son. Pappy begs too hard for me to go with him that fin'ly they lets me. I never seed my mammy after that, bein' as how Missy Emogene stays in Alabama and us come to Texas.

"Massa George settles near Gilmer and he sho' have a big place with lots of acres and a good house. He didn't 'low no beatin' on that place but I've saw slaves on other places whopped till the blood run off them onto the groun'. When they was cut loose from the tree or whippin' post they falls over like dead. But our massa was good to us and give us lots to eat and wear. We et pork meat and white flour jest like the white folks and every woman have to spin so many yards cloth 'fore she go to bed, so we allus had the clothes.

"I've saw lots of slaves bid off like stock and babies sold from their mammy's breast. Some brung 'bout $1,500, owing to how strong they is. Spec'lators used to ride all over the country near our place and buy up niggers and I've saw as many as fifty in a gang, like convicts.

Reeves Tucker

"But Massa George wouldn't sell and buy slaves and none of 'em ever run off 'cept my pappy and one night he started to go 'cross a shirt of woods to the neighbors and young massa was a pattyroller and tells pappy to wait and go with him, but pappy hard headed as a mule and goes hisself and the pattyrollers cotches him and nigh beats him to death. Young massa was sho' mad as fire, 'cause he didn't want his niggers beat up.

"Them circuit ridin' preachers come to the white church and tries to make the white folks bring their slaves to preaching. Preacher say, 'Nigger have a soul to save same as us all.' Massa allus went to church but I don't 'lieve it done him any good, 'cause while he there at meetin' the niggers in the field stacking that fodder. He did give us Christmas Day and a big dinner and 'cept for workin' the lights outten us, gen'rally treated us decent and we had heap easier time than any other slaves 'round.

"I 'member the war and Jeff Davis and Abe Lincoln was warfaring 'bout freein' the niggers 'bout four year 'fore they fought. Massa Tucker jest grunted when we was freed, 'cause he knowed the thing was up, and he tells us if we'd stay and help the crop out he'd give us a horse and saddle, but we didn't git nothin'. So I lef' him soon as the crop laid by the year of freedom and then moved with pappy to a farm near Hallsville and stays with him till I marries. I had seven chillen to be growed and married and I farmed near Hallsville mos' my life, till I too old. My son, Reeves after me, owns this farm and we's all right. Never did have hard times after freedom, like some niggers, 'cause we just sot down on the land."

LOU TURNER

Lou Turner, 89, was born at Rosedale, near Beaumont, Texas, on the Richard West plantation. She has spent her entire life within three miles of Beaumont, and now lives in her own little home, with her daughter, Sarah.

"I hears you been 'round to see me befo', but you ain't never gwine find me to home. I sho' love to go 'round visitin'. You know dey say iffen you treats the cat too good, you ain't never know where the cat is.

"I's gwine on seventeen year old when freedom come. I's born right here near Beaumont, on the big road what they calls the Concord Road, in the place what they calls Rosedale. I's a growed-up young lady befo' I ever sees Beaumont. I's gwine on 89 year old now.

"Richard West, he's my massa and Mary Guidry she my missy. Dey used to call her the 'Cattle King.' Dey have a big plantation and jes' a few slaves. Dey raises my mammy since she eleven year old. Her name Maria and she marry Sam Marble. He come from Miss'ippi.

"I stay up at the big house and missy fix my plate when she fix hers. God bless her heart, she kind to me, I know now I's sassy to her but she didn't pay me no 'tention 'cause I's li'l. I slep' on a trundle bed by missy's side and I git so smart I allus smell my bed to see iffen dey puts nice, clean sheets on mine like dey did on hers. Sometime I play sick, but old missy a good doctor and she gimme beefoot oil and it so nasty I quit playing off. She French and she so good doctor they send for her to other folks houses.

"Old missy was real rich. I's taken her money out of de wardrobe ane make tall playhouse out of gold and silver money. Iffen she have to buy somethin' she have to come and borrow it from me. Us allus has to figger how to take dat money out of de corners so de house won't fall down. I cried and cried iffen she tored it up.

"She'd take me with her when she go to see her grandchillen in de French settlement. Us come in buggy or hack and bring jelly and money and things. I thought I's gwine to Heaven, 'cause I gits to play with li'l chillen. Us play 'ring place', dat's draw a ring and hop 'round in it. Us jump rope and swing. Dey have a hair rope swing with a smooth board in it so it ain't scratch us behin'.

"Old missy so kind but what got 'way with me, I couldn't go to school. I beg and beg, but she kep' sayin', 'Some day, some day,' and I ain't never sit in a school in my life.

"Old massa didn't work 'em hard. He make 'en come in when the sun got bad, 'cause he feared dey git sunstroke. He mighty good in early days, but when he figger dey gwine loose he slaves he start bein' mean. He split 'em and sold 'em, tryin' to make he money out of 'em.

"De house what the white folks live in was make out of logs and moss and so was the quarters houses. Better'n New Orleans, dem quarters was. Us slaves have de garden patch. The white folks raises hogs and kilt 'em by the twenties. Dey smoke hams and shoulders and chittlin's and sich and hang 'em up in the smokehouse. Us allus have plenty to eat and us have good, strong clothes. Missy buy my dresses separate, though. She buy me pretty stripe cotton dress.

"Bout the only work I ever done was help watch the geese and turkeys and fill the quilts. I larn to card, too. Old missy never whip me much, she jes' like to scare me. She whip me with big, tall straw she git out the field or wet a towel and whip my legs. My old massa done a trick I never forgit while I's warm. I's big gal 'bout sixteen year old and us all 'lone on the place. He tells me to crawl under the corncrib and git the eggs. I knowed dey ain't nothin' dere but the nest egg, but I have to go. When I can't find nothin' he pull me out backwards by the feet and whip me. When old missy come home I ain't know no better'n to tell her and she say she ought to kill him, but she sho' fix him, anyway. He say she spile me and dat why he whip me.

"Old missy taken to preachin'. She was real good preacher. Dey have de big hall down the center of the house where they have services. A circuit rider come once a month and everybody stop workin' even if it wasn't Sunday.

Lou Turner

"When war was on us there wasn't no sojers 'round where I was, but dat battle on Atchafalia shook all the dishes off the dresser and broke 'em up. Jes' broke up all the fine Sunday and company dishes.

"After de trouble my mammy have gettin' me 'way from there when freedom come, she gits me after all. Old missy have seven li'l nigger chillen what belong to her slaves, but dey mammies and daddys come git 'em. I didn't own my own mammy. I own my old missy and call her 'mama'. Us cry and cry when us have to go with us mammy. I 'members how old missy rock me in her arms and sing to me. She sing dat 'O, Susanna' and telt me a story:

"'Dere a big, old brown bear what live in de woods and she have lots of li'l cub bears and dey still nussin' at de breast. Old mama bear she out huntin' one day and she come by de field where lots of darkies workin' and dere on a pallet she see fat, li'l pickaninny baby. Mama bear she up and stole dat li'l pickaninny baby and takes it home. It hongry but after she git all de cub bears fed, dere ain't no milk left for de nigger baby. Mama bear git so 'sasperated she say to her babies, 'Go long, you go way and play.' Dan she feed de li'l pickaninny baby and dat how she raise dat nigger baby.'

"Now, every time old missy come to dat place in de story, she start laughin', 'cause I allus used to ask her.

"'How come dey didn't no hair grow on dat baby.'"

IRELLA BATTLE WALKER

Irella Battle Walker, 86, was born a slave at Craft's Prairie, Texas. Her parents, Mesheck and Becky Battle, belonged to Mr. Battle, but were sold while Irella was a baby to Tom Washington, of Travis County. Irella learned her A B C's from an old slave, Jack James, although it was against the rules. This was the only schooling she ever had. Irella receives a monthly old age pension of eight dollars. She lives at 2902 Cole St., Austin, Texas.

"My name was Irella Battle and I was borned on August 15th, in 1851, down at Craft's Prairie, in Bastrop County. I was 86 years old last August, and I'm blind in one eye.

"Mammy's name was Becky Battle and she was a field worker, and dat about de most work she have to do, 'cept on rainy days. She had five girls and one boy and I'm de youngest and de only livin' one now. Daddy was Mesheck Battle and when I'm a baby in mammy's arms, us sold to Massa Washington.

"Daddy had to do field work. I never knowed him do nothin' but farm. He sho' make us behave and whop us if we didn't. Massa was purty good. De massas dem times, some was good and some was bad, and about de most of dem was bad. I had to he'p round de big house and dey purty good to me. But when I still little I went to de fields.

Dey give me a sack what de slaves make to pick cotton in. Dey spin de thread and make cloth on de loom and stitch it and make cotton sacks. Dey short for us chillen and de older folks had a short one to pick in and a big sack to empty in. I could pick about a hundred fifty pounds a day when I's twelve. Israel Roberts could pick five hundred a day. Us never got no money for pickin', only food and clothes and a place to stay at night. Old man Jonas watched us chillen and kept us divin' for dat cotton all de day long. Us wish him dead many a time.

"De plantation had a hoss-power gin and some days our rows of cotton tooked us right to de gin house and we'd look up and watch de slave boys settin' on de lever and drivin' dem hosses round and round.

"De cabins was log and mud and stick chimney. When one dem chimneys catch fire us git on top and throw water on it.

"In summer us go barefoot, but dere shoemakers what make shoes for winter. When a beef killed, de hide kept and cleaned and put in de tannin' trough. When de leather ready, de shoes make in de little shoe shop, and when dem shoes git dry dey hard as a rock. Daddy make us rub tallow or fried grease meat or any other kind grease into dat hard shoe leather, and it make dem soft, but when de dew and sun git on dem again dey's hard again. Times de coyotes steal dem greased shoes and make off with dem. Dat act'ly happen a lot of times.

"Old man Jack James work at day and have night school at night. He have long boards for benches and let dem down by ropes from de rafters, and have blue back spellers. He point to de letters with de long broom straw and dat's how we larn our A B C's. I can read purty good, when my eyes let me, but I can't write nothin'.

"If it rained we had to shuck and shell corn or pull weeds in de yard, and it was a big one, too. De women spin thread for de looms, two of dem and a spinnin' wheel in every cabin.

"Us have beds de men make and take wore out clothes and breeches and piece dem and stuff with cotton for quilts. When it cold us keep fire all night long. De plates am tin and a big gourd dipper to drink water with. De men make dere own cedar water pails.

"De week's rations for a growed person run like three pounds bacon and a peck cornmeal and some homemade 'lasses. No flour and no coffee, but us parch bran or wheat and make coffee. Each night dey give a pint of sweet milk. But de chillen all et in a special place in de kitchen.

"One mornin' Massa Washington call us all and he read from de big paper. He say, 'You is free to live and free to die and free to go to de devil, if you wants to.' He tell us if we gather he crops he'd pay us for it. Den he turned and walked away and started cryin'. All de families stays but one man. De highest price massa pay anybody was about $15.00, but dat seem like a lot of money to folks what wasn't used to gittin' any money at all.

"Finally my folks moved on a farm on Onion Creek, in Travis County, on rented land from Nat Watters and Dr. Shears, and farm on de third and fourth. We stays about six years and raises cotton and corn.

"But when I's twenty years old I marries Joe Walker

and us move to Bastrop County, add I stays dere till he dies in 1932. Us have eleven chillen and nine of dem still livin'. I gits a pension, nine dollars de month, and it sho' am a help now I's old and nearly blind."

JOHN WALTON

John Walton, 87, was born August 15, 1849, a slave of Bill Walton, who lived in Austin, Texas, until the Civil War. He then purchased a farm in Robertson County, Texas. John and his wife, Missouri, own a little home at 1008 Juniper St., Austin. Each receives an old age pension of $10.00 a month.

"My name am John Walton, yes, suh, and I's born right here in Austin. Dat on de 15th day of August, in 1849. I done had de papers on dat but where dey is now I don't know. Pappy's named Gordon Walton and I 'member he die while de war goin' on, or jes' befo'. I disremember. My mammy was a small woman, named Mary.

"Massa Bill Walton owns all us, and he de brother of Buck Walton, and us live in Austin till it said de Yankees comin'. Some southern folks here in Austin was diggin' ground for a fort, old Fort MacGruder, jes' south of Austin. So Massa Bill takes us all 'way from Austin and up to Robertson County, 'cause he done figured de Yankees can't git up dere.

"I done field work up dere and even us kids had to pick 150 pounds cotton a day, or git de whoppin'. Us puts de cotton in de white-oak baskets and some dem hold more'n 100 pounds. It 'cordin' to de way you stamps you cotton in. De wagon with de yoke of oxen standin' in de field for to pour de cotton in and when it full, de oxen pulls dat wagon to de hoss-power gin. Us gin'rally use 'bout 1,600 pounds cotton to make de bale.

"Purty soon after Massa Walton opens he farm he die and Missus Walton den marries a Dr. Richardson and he git de overseer what purty rough on us. He want all us to stay right in line and chop 'long and keep up with de lead man. If us didn't it am de bullwhip. He ride up and down and hit us over de back if us don't do de job right. Sometimes he'd git off he hoss and have two slaves hold one down and give him de bullwhip. He'd give it to him, too.

"I helped break up de land and plant and chop cotton and a little of everything. Jes' what had to be done at de time, I goes out and does it. I run 'cross plenty snakes and one day one bit me right top de foot. Dere plenty varmints, too.

"In de fall of de year us kill plenty hawgs and put up de gamblin' racks and hang dat meat up for de night. Dere some big dogs what watched de meat and one old dog, old Jefferson, was bigger'n any dog I ever seed. He kilt many 'nother dog. One night a big panther try steal de hawg meat and old Jeff cotch him and helt him till de men comes. De panther tore Jeff up purty bad. Us heered dem panthers scream at night, and if you didn't know, you'd think it a woman. I could tell de diff'rence, 'cause de panther scream have de little growl at de end. If he half mile 'way, you'd hear dat little whang.

"One night I goes out in de bottom with my dog. I was huntin' but I don't like what I finds. A big panther follows me and old Nig, dat my big, black bulldog, scart him 'way from me. I sho' run dat night, and I never slip 'way no more at night.

"Massa's big house sot 'way from our cabins. Us have de big room where de slaves' meals all cook and de fireplace 'bout four foot 'cross and plenty ashes in de mornin' to make de ashcakes. For breakfast us have meat and ashcakes and bran-coffee or sassafras tea. You could keep dem dried sassafras roots de year 'round and dey jes' as strong. Us plowed 'em up in de field, 'cause dey growed wild.

"Us didn't have time for de playin' of games durin' de week, 'cause it dark when us goes out and it dark when us comes back. Us sho' was tired. At night dat overseer walk by our cabins and call out to us, to see if us all inside. If us don't answer he come up and find out why, and he'd find us, too.

"I larned to read and write a little jes' since freedom. Us used Webster's old blue-back spellers and I has one in de house to dis day and I wouldn't take nothing for it.

"The first year after freedom I farms with mammy and my stepdaddy. Pappy done die. Us done purty good de first year and I keeps on farmin' most my life. I marries Georgia Anne Harper in 1875 or 1876 in Limestone County. Us have four chillen and three is livin'. I marries 'gain in 1882 to Missouri Fisher and us have eight chillen and six is livin'.

"Us gits 'long on what de state give us now, and it ain't so bad. Times is diff'rent. I never done much but farm, so I don't know so much 'bout everything what goes on."

SOL WALTON

Sol Walton, 88, was born in Mobile, Alabama, a slave of Sam Lampkin. Sol and his father stayed on the Lampkin Plantation, then in Mooringsport, Louisiana, until 1873, and farmed on shares. From 1876 to 1922 Sol worked in the T.& P. shops, in Marshall, Texas. Sol and his wife are supported by odd jobs Sol secures about town and they receive money from a son who is in a CCC camp.

"I was knockin' round, a good-sized chap, way back yonder in Buchanan's and Henry Clay's time. I was born in 1849, in Mobile, Alabama, and belonged to Sam Lampkin. My father was bought by the Lampkins and he allus kept the name of his first master, Walton. My mammy was a Alabama Negro and her name was Martha, and I had four brothers and four sisters, Robert, Jim, Richard, Alex, Anna, Dora, Isabella, Bettie.

"My master was Sam Lampkin and his wife was Missus Mary, and their first plantation was in Alabama, but they moved to Mississippi when I was 'bout six, and we lived on Salt Water Creek. They had a big, frame house and we lived in log quarters, slept on rough rail beds and had plenty to eat, peas, pumpkins, rice and other truck we raised on the place, and plenty of fish out of the creek.

"The first work I done in slavery was totin' water and

dinner to the field hands, in gourd buckets. We didn't have tin buckets then. The hands worked from sun to sun, and if the overseer seed 'em slackin' up he cussed 'em and sometimes whacked 'em with a bullwhip. I seed 'em whipped till their shirt stuck to their back. I seed my mammy whipped for shoutin' at white folks meetin'. Old massa stripped her to the waist and whipped her with a bullwhip. Heaps of 'em was whipped jus' 'cause they could be whipped. Some owners half fed their hands and then whipped them for beggin' for grub.

"After our folks came in from the field they et supper and some went to Salt Water Creek to cotch fish and crabs. They used to spin at night, too. On Christmas Day massa allus give the slaves a little present, mostly somethin' to wear, 'cause he goin' to git that anyhow.

"Massa never had but one white overseer. He got kilt fightin'. The hands was burnin' logs and trash and the overseer knocked a old man down and made some of the niggers hold him while he bullwhipped him. The old man got up and knocked the overseer in the head with a big stick and then took a ax and cut off his hands and feet. Massa said he didn't ever want another white overseer and he made my cousin overlooker after that.

"The slaves had their own prayer meetin's and that's 'bout the biggest pleasure they had. We'd slip off sometimes to dances and parties, but the patterrollers come and run us home with hounds. The black and white children all played together and there was 'bout sixty of us.

"The old folks told us ghost stories but I never seed a ghost but once, after I was married. Me and some men was walkin' down the Shreveport road and saw a big house all lit up and fiddlin' and dancin' goin' on inside. But when we got close the music stops and the lights went out. When we got on past a piece it lit up and the fiddlin' starts 'gain. I wasn't scared, but we didn't hang round to see what made it do that way.

"Some of the cullud folks on our place could read and write. They larned it theyselves. The white folks didn't larn 'em. All they larned 'em was to work hard. But they took care of us when we was sick and old women made lots of medicine. There was boneset tea and willow tea and shuck tea and cottonseed tea for chills and fever and Jerusalum Oak for worms.

Sol Walton

"Master left Mississippi for Texas 'bout time the war got goin' good, with his fam'ly and sixty slaves. We'd been on the road three weeks when a gang of Yankees come on us one day at dinner. The niggers scatters like birds. 'Bout half of 'em never come back, but the rest of us come on and settled seven miles southwest of Mooringsport, in Louisiana. Young master went to the war after we got there and come home sev'ral times. But they didn't talk the war 'mongst us cullud folks.

"Nothin' special happened the day they said we was free, 'cept some of 'em didn't stay ten minutes. Master told 'em if they'd stay he'd give them the third and fourth. The ones who left wasn't promised nothin' and didn't git nothin'. My folks stayed for 'most twenty years after 'mancipation, workin' on the halves.

"I left my folks in '73 and come to Jimmie D. Scott's place, in Texas, 'bout eight miles east of Marshall, and worked for $10.00 the month. That's where I met Liza Montecue, who is my wife. She was born on the Scott's place the same year I was born. We moved to Marshall in '76 and I got a job in the railroad shops and worked till the big strike in 1922. I didn't belong to the strike but the strikers wouldn't let me work. After they run me off my job, I never could get back on and had to make a livin' at anythin' I could find till my boy got in the CCC camp. I been married sixty-four years and raised eight children, and three of 'em lives here and works at anythin' they can find to make a dollar."

ELLA WASHINGTON

Ella Washington, 82, was born a slave of Dave Mann, in St. Mary's Parish, Louisiana. When the slaves were freed in Louisiana Ella was taken to Calvert, Texas, and put on the Barton plantation. Soon after the civil war she came to Galveston, and lives with her daughter, who supports herself and her mother by taking in washing.

"You got to 'scuse how I looks, 'cause I been out in de back yard helpin' my daughter with de washin'. She allus fuss at me 'cause I work like dat, but I tells her jes' 'cause I is a old woman ain't no reason why I got to act like one.

"I don't know for sho' jes' when I'm birthed, but my sister allus say I's one year and six months older'n her and she say she's birthed 'bout 1857. Dey didn't make no record den like now. I thinks old massa, Dave Mann, keep some kind record on us, but he been dead de long time.

"My mammy and pappy was name Meine, Car'line and Charles Meine. De slaves used to take de massa's name and sometimes when dey sold dey drap de old name and take de new massa's name. Dat how come it so hard to keep up with dem.

"Massa Mann sho' nice but him and he missy die and Massa Jim Ross step into dere shoes on de plantation. Us gits swamp den. When you git swamp dat mean you got to live with a mean man. He sho' was mean, too.

"De plantation was big and 'bout a hundred slaves on it. Dey work dem hard, too, sometimes till nine o'clock at night. A lot of dem run away but dey sic de nigger dogs on dere trail and cotch dem. When dey cotch dem dey whup dem. Dey put sticks in de ground and tie dere hands and feet to dem. Some places dey strip dem naked and whip dem.

"Sometimes Massa Jim 'low us go to de Catholic Church at Marion. Dey wouldn't 'low us to pray by ourself. But we sneaks off and have pot prayin'. Two men carry de great big hog pot dey uses to scald hogs and take it out in de woods and us stick de head in it and pray. All de noise go in de pot and you couldn't hear it outside.

"Old massa fed us good, meal and syrup and meat 'nough to last. He give us watermelons every Sunday. But Massa Jim didn't 'lieve in pamperin' niggers, he say. He didn't give us much to eat and de houses leak 'cause de walls rotten.

"One time he take de notion to sell us. He put my mother and me and sister on de block up in Marion. Us all cryin' hard, 'cause us thunk us gwine git sep'rate. Den I looks up sudden and right at my young miss, Miss Mary. She so mad she pale like de ghost. She say, 'Ella, you git 'way from dat block and come over to me, and you too, Della.' Me and my sister runs over dere to her and wrop ourself round her dress and hold on with all our might. De massa come after us and Miss Mary say, 'What you mean sellin' my slaves?' He say us slaves his and she say, do he want to have to prove what he say. Den she start in and raise so much sand he have to call mammy down off de block and take us back home.

"I heared everybody say a war goin' on and my uncle and cousin run 'way to de head bureau, where de Yankees at. My mammy say it at Milligan, Texas. Time dey ready for freedom in Louisiana, dey refugees us to Texas, in de wagons. Us travel all day and half de night and sleep on de ground. It ain't take us so long to git to Calvert, out dere in de bottom of Texas, and dey puts us on de Barton plantation. We's diggin' potatoes dere when de Yankees come up with two big wagons and make us come out of de fields and free us. Dere wasn't no cel'bration 'bout it. Massa say us can stay couple days till us 'cide what to do.

"Well, den somethin' funny happen dere. De slaves all drinks out an old well. Dey'd drink water in de mornin' and dey'd have de cramps awful bad 'bout dinner time and in de evenin' dey's dead. Dey dies like flies, so fast dey couldn't make de coffins for dem. Dey jes' sew dem up in sacks and bury dem dat way. Some de slaves say massa put de poison in de well. I don't know what kill dem but it sho' look funny.

"Mammy and me goes to Calvert and hires out, but 'fore long us come to Galveston and pappy go back to Louisiana. If he ain't dead he still live dere in St. Mary's Parish. I never seen him no more.

"I marries 'bout 1886, and stays right here in Galveston. I seen Wright Cuney lots of times but I ain't never knowed him to talk to. I 'member when dey say he be governor some day, but dey ain't gwine have no cullud man governor. Course, he did git to congress."

ROSA WASHINGTON

Rosa Washington is 90 years old and lives in her own little adobe house at 3911 Manzana St., El Paso, Texas. She was born a slave of the Watson family, on a large plantation seven miles from St. Joe, Louisiana. Her parents came from Georgia. After the Civil War she left her former owners, but later returned and was with them until they died. She came to Texas in 1921, and her three children provide for her. Her son, Le Roy, has been in the U.S. Emigration service in El Paso for 27 years.

"My name's Rosa Washington and my husban' was Joe Washington. He's been dead a long time. I was bo'n on a big plantation, white man's name Bill Watson, wife Ann Watson, seven miles from St. Joe. Mama had four chillen and I had seven. Marster had a fine house and plenty of slaves. I dunno how many.

"'Fore we was free we was in the fiel' workin' and they come out and got us. Everybody threw up their hands and started to run. The Yanks busted open a sugar hogshead and give everybody all they wanted. Dey threw all de milk away and dey carried our marster away by force and tuk him to jail in Vicksburg. Our missus wept. When the Yankees got us, dey tuk us about three miles from whar we live, put us in a fine house, give us plenty to eat until war's ended. Me and my chillen and my father and mother were together there.

"We had a good cabin on the plantation, made out-a planks, ole rip-rap plunder. Dey treated us good. I worked in water garden, worked in fiel's when 10 years old. Hoe'd my row every day. Dey didn' whop me, though. My mistress wouldn' let 'em. Marsa and missus good to me. I not tell lie on 'em. Tell truf. Truf shines.

"I seed niggers put in stocks, put 'em in stocks head in fust. Tear their clothes off backs, whop till sores come, den dey pour coal oil and turpentine in sores. I see dat with my own eyes. My dad druv the carriage, carried 'em 'round all time. My mother worked in the fiel' like I do. Work every day. Dey give us everything to eat. Marster and missus, too, give plenty, but if ole cow died with cholera, they give to us niggers. I got good shoes once a year. When marster went to New Orleans, mama had to tie my feet up in rags. I had to work with the rest of 'em. Got up at 4 o'clock. We he'ped on other plantations when dey'd git behind. Go he'p 'em out.

"I waited on overseers table, Joe Crusa. He was mean. He stuck a fork in my head. Ole Aunt Clarissie cooked for us. She cook in cabin for us, had big fireplace. She cook for all niggers on the place. She was mean to me, never married. She had two rooms, all she do was cook, tell lies on me to white overseer. That woman told a lie on me 'cause said I lef' a fork dirty. He look at it, says, 'Who rubbed dis fork?' Woman says, 'Rosa,' and he stuck the fork in my head. Missus turn him off nex' day.

"We had co'nbread, no sugar, plenty okra and coffee; plenty milk, 'cause they had 17 cows. They give us clabber and peaches. Every day overseer blow horn in yard to wake us up, a bugle at four o'clock Sundays. We take cotton outta fiel' and put it up on scaffold to dry iffen it rain. Overseer sit in dry, big overcoat on; we work in mud and rain. One mornin' they carried us to stockhouse to whip us. My missus and marster never let 'em whip me, but no white folks he'p me to read and write. He'p me to do nothin' but work.

"White folks had church. I couldn' go. I hadda mind the white chillen every Sunday. Cullud people had to go way back in woods to have church. Never let white folks see 'em. Had to slip and hide to have our church, run like deer if foun' out. Marster never know a bit more'n this chair whar we was gwine. He couldn' ask us on Sunday, it be against the law. Iffen niggers run away, dogs 'ud catch 'em.

"Dey had doctor right dere. Kep' us well. Kep' us well so's we could work. Brother-in-law to marster.

"When the niggers was married, dey put a broom down and dey jump over the broom, same time missus and marster'd marry 'em. He'd marry 'em and she as witness. Sometimes celebrate. She'd cook 'em some cake, give 'em a fine dress. We'd take meat and skillets down to the bar on Sundays. Had fish frys. Wouldn' take no fussy chillen to the bar. We chillen would have fish fry whar dey couldn't watch us.

"Had to go to gin at four o'clock in evenin'. Couldn' play week-days, had to go in cabin and be still. Never got to play much till Yankees come and got us, but we had a big ball and dance in yard Christmas. Had candy, dey give us dresses and socks and a good feast for Christmas.

Give us things for 4th of July. Dey give us dat day. No, dey wouldn' whip us dat day. We had a big quiltin' Christmas day. We'd piece de quilts outta scraps. Some couldn' quilt. Dey'd dance in de yard all day.

"We niggers got wool clothes in winter, good clothes woven on de place. Marster had black sheep and white sheep. He bought our summer clothes in New Orleans—linsey, calicy, plaid, some white ones. Dey'd give us color what we like.

Rosa Washington

"Sure, I seed ghosts. Dey come with no head, come outta de fiel' one night so late, 'bout eight, nine o'clock. I was scared, yes, suh, I sure was scared, but my mammy say, 'Dey ain' goin' to hurt you, baby.' Dey scare me. My mammy give me beads for my neck, china-berry beads to keep me well. They's pretty. I never had no other kind.

"We never git no money befo' freedom. I stay away from Marster and missus de first year, den go back. Dey give us 50¢ a day after war. Had to pay for rations. Better since war, though. No whippin's goin' on like they did 'fore.

"I'se a full Baptist—been ever since '67. I'se happy. Sometimes I gits too happy. I don' move till de spirit move me. I goes to church when I'se able. But I'se gittin' too old to go now—I'se just waitin' to go home."

SAM JONES WASHINGTON

Sam Jones Washington, 88, was born a slave of Sam Young, who owned a ranch along the Colorado River, in Wharton Co., Texas. Sam was trained to be a cowhand, and worked for his master until 1868, receiving wages after he was freed. He farmed until 1905, then moved to Fort Worth and worked in the packing plants until 1931. He lives at 3520 Columbus Ave., Fort Worth, and is supported by an $11.00 per month old age pension, supplemented by what Sam raises in his garden and makes out of a few hogs.

"How old I is? I's 16 year when surrender come. I knows dat, 'cause of massa's statement. All us niggers gits de statement when surrender come. I's seed plenty slave days.

"Massa Young run de small farm 'long de Colorado River and him don't own many slaves. Dere my mammy and her six chillen, and Majoria and her four chillens. My pappy am not on de place. I don't know my pappy. Him am what dey calls de travelin' nigger. Dey have him come for service and when dey gits what dey wants, he go back to he massa. De womens on Massa Young place not married.

"Massa raise jes' a little cotton, dat two womens and de chillen could tend to, and some veg'tables and sich. Us have lots of good food. Us sleep in de sleepin' room, nex' to massa's house, but I sleeps in massa's room.

"One night massa say, 'Don't tie my hoss to de stake tonight.' But I's sleepy and gits de nodfies and draps off to sleep. Mammy shake me and say, 'Did you stake de hoss?' Massa sees dat hoss in de mornin' and say, 'You done stake dat hoss and I told you not to.' He gives me couple licks and I larns to do what I's told. He never whip nobody, not de hard whippin' like other niggers gits. He am de good massa.

"I fust runs errands and den massa larn me to ride, soon's I could sit de hoss. Den I stays out with de cattle mos' de time and I's tickled. I sho' likes to ride and rope dem cattle and massa allus fix me up with good clothes and good hoss and good saddle. I stays dere till long after surrender.

"Us have stampedes from de cattle. Dat am cust'mary with dem critters. Dat mean ride de hoss to turn de cattle. Us ride to side de leader and crowd him and force him to turn, and keep forcin' him, and by and by dem critters am runnin' in de circle. Dat keep dem from scatterment. Dat sho' dangerous ridin'. If de hoss throw you off dem cattle stamp you to death. Gabriel sho' blow he horn for you den!

"I sho' 'joys dat business, 'cause we'uns have de good time. Us go to town and have fun. One time I comes near gittin' in trouble, but it ain't my fault. I's in town and massa, too, and a white man come to me and him show de drink. 'Who you 'long to, nigger?' he say. 'I's Massa Young's nigger,' I says, polite-like. 'You looks like de smart nigger and I's de notion smack you one,' he say.

'You better not smack me any,' I says. You unnerstand, dat de way massa raise me. I don't unnerstand some cruel white mens gits de arg'ment, jus' for de chance to shoot de nigger. Massa am standin' near by and him come up and say, 'If you touches dat nigger, I'll put de bullet through you.' Dat man see massa have no foolishment in he words and gits gwine. But if massa am not dere, Gabriel blow he horn for dis nigger's Jubilee, right den, yes, sar.

Sam Jones Washington

"I comes near gittin' cotched by de patterrollers once. I's jus' 12 den and 'nother nigger and me, us want some cane stalk. It good to eat raw, you knows. Jus' peel de bark off and chew dat inside. Well, we'uns in de man's cane patch, breakin' dem stalks and dey makes de poppin' noise. A patterroller come by and hear dat poppin', and holler, 'Who's dere in de cane patch?' Us didn't answer him, no, sar. I 'cides right quick dat I don't like cane and I comes 'way from dat patch. I outsmarts and outruns dat patterroller. I keeps to de cane fields and de woods and I runs dis way and dat way. I twists 'round so he couldn't follow my tracks. Like de snake's track, you can't tell if it am gwine north or comin' back. Lawd a'mighty! How fast I runs. I stays 'head of my shadow. I tells you, I's a-gwine!

"De war? White man, we'uns didn't know dere am de war. We seed some sojers at de start, but dat all. One day massa say to me, 'After dis, you gits $15.00 de month wages. I works for him three more years and den he sold out. Den I goes farmin' till 1905. I works in de packin' plants here in Fort Worth den, till I's wore out, 'bout six year ago. Now I raises de hawgs, not very many, and does what work I can git. Dat pension from de State sho' holps me. With dat and de hawgs and de little garden I gits by, and so I lives.

"Was I ever marry? Man, man, three time. Fust time, 'bout 1869 and we'uns gits de seperment in 1871. Dat woman sho' deal me mis'ry! She am de troublin' woman. Den 'bout 1873 I marries 'gain and she die 'fore long. Den in 1905 I marries 'gain and she's dead, too. I never has de chillen. I's jus' 'lone and old now, and stay here till my time comes. I 'spect it quite a spell yit, 'cause I's got lots of substance left, yes, sar."

WILLIAM WATKINS

William Watkins, born 1850, to Julia and Hudson Watkins. All were slaves on the Watkins plantation where William was born, on the edge of Charlotte County, Virginia. William is tall, heavy set, and does not look his age. He lives with William Branch, who came from an adjoining county in Virginia. Both men served in the same campaigns in the United States Army.

"My name is William Watkins. De name comes frum de name of Terbaccer Watkins, who owned de Watkins Terbaccer Plantation. He got a factory in Richmond and de plantation in Charlotte County in Virginia, 'bout 50 mile east of Richmond. Marse Watkins got a big frame house and 400 acres and 100 acres is terbaccer. Yassuh, dey's other crops—barley, wheat, oats, and den dey's stock—hogs, cows, hosses and mules.

"We lives in log cabins wid plank floors and we made de beds ourself. Dey feeds us good and we gits milk and bread and lotsa pork. Marse Watkins got lotsa hawgs.

"Yassuh, we's got a church. De slaves built it in de woods. We never got no wages but sometimes he give us four bits or six bits. What we do wid it? We buys candy. Sometimes we run de rabbits or goes fishing. De Marster gives us lil' patches of groun'. He's good but de overseer's rough. He whips all de slaves.

"Dey's a patrol what watches for slaves dat runs away, but we don't have no patrol on our plantation. We has dances Sat'day nights. Sundays we didn't wuk much.

"Dey's ghosts dere—we seed 'em. Dey's w'ite people wid a sheet on 'em to scare de slaves offen de plantation. We wears charms to keep us well. Dere's asafoetida in a bag and we wear's it roun' de neck. It cure most ev'ryting. When we gits real sick, dey sends medicine frum de big house.

"Ev'ry year de slave traders comes and de Marster sells some slaves down river to New Orleans. Who dey sell? Jes' no count slaves. Dey walks all de way. De traders dey rides in ox-carts. We never wuk much Sundays, only to milk de cows. Jes' dat. Yessuh, I was married on de plantation. De preacher say de words and we's married.

"Den de war come and de Yankees come down thick as leaves. Dey burns de big house and de slave houses and ev'ryting. Dey turns us loose. We ain't got no home nor nuthin' to eat, 'cause dey tells us we's free.

"We's gotta leave de plantation. De Marster's gone, de crops is gone, de stock's gone. We goes to anudder place and works on shares. De first time we sees de Ku Klux is right after de war. Dey whips de slaves what leaves de plantations, dey don' wan' dem to be free.

"Bout 1870 I goes to Ohio and enlists in de army at Jefferson Barracks and right off dey sends us to Texas to fight Indians. I goes to San Antonio and dey puts me on guard at de Alamo to fight off de Indians. Den I goes to Fort Davis. I'm in de cullud Indian Scouts, Co. K, and dey's a banker name of Miller in de Chihuahua jail. One night de kuhnel takes us from Fort Davis, and we marches all night wid guns and 150 rounds of ammunition in belts, and rations for 30 days. We marches all night long twel we gits to Del Norte, Texas(Presidio) and we crosses de river and takes Mr. Miller out of jail.

William Watkins

"While we's at Fort Davis a wagon train comes through de canyon and de Apaches rolls big rocks down on de white people and kills 26 of dem. Dey scalps all dey kills and we go out and fit de Apaches. De lieutenant is killed in de fight. Yassuh, we fit Apaches all de time and when we goes to Fort Concho dey gives us a fit all 'long de road. Den we fitten de Cheyennes and dey is wust of all. Dey's great big Indians 'bout seven feet tall and at de battle of de Wichita in de Indian Territory a Cheyenne shoots an arrer through my wrist. (He exhibited the scar. Same battle described in interview with Wm. Branch.)

"Den after my wound heals we's sent to Fort Clark and de sergeant, Jeff Walker, got it in for me. Kuhnel Andrews is at Fort Davis and Jeff Walker trumps up some charges dat I'se mistrusted, so dey gives me a dishonnuble discharge 'cause of dat Jeff Walker. I ain't had no court martial nor no trial and I cain't git no pension 'count of de dishonnuble discharge.

"And now I'se strong and well but I cain't git no wuk 'cause I'se so ole. And 'cause Jeff Walker didn't like me, I gits a dishonnuble discharge."

DIANAH WATSON

Dianah Watson, 102, was born a slave of Tom Williams, at New Orleans. In 1870, Dianah went to Jefferson, Texas. She now lives with a married daughter in the Macedonia Community, five miles northwest of Marshall, Tex.

"My name am Dianah Watson and I used to keep my age, but I done got sick and can't 'member it now. I can't say 'zactly how old I is but I's a past-growed woman when the war broke out, and my old missy's daughter done told me once out the book I's borned in 1835.

"I's borned and bred 'bout a half mile from New Orleans. My mammy was s*arah Hall and she's borned in Galveston, and my papa was Bill Williams. My old missy done take me from my mammy when I's a small baby and raised me to a full-growed woman. I slep' in the same room with my young missy and had a good time in slavery, didn't suffer for nothin' and never was cut and slashed like some. Me and Miss Laura come right up together and I's her own nigger slave.

"Massa Williams treated his black folks with 'spect. They was in the field from 'fore day till dark, but they was took good care of and fed and plenty clothes. Old Master Tom done the bossin' hisself and when he's dyin' he calls all his five boys to his bed and say, 'Boys, when I's gone,

I don't want no cuttin' and slashin' my niggers. They's got feelin' same as us.'

"But the oldes' boy, William, got the debbil in him and hires a overseer, and he rid in the fields with a quirt and rope and chair on his saddle. When he done take a notion to whip a nigger, he'd make some the men tie that nigger to the chair and beat him somethin' scand'lous. He got mad at my mother's sister, Aunt Susie Ann, and beat her till the blood run off her on the ground. She fall at his feets like she passed out and he put up the whip and she trips him and gits the whip and whips him till he couldn't stand up. Then some the niggers throwed him off a cliff and broke his neck. His folks gits the sheriff but master's boys orders him off the place with a gun. There warn't no more overseers on the place after that.

"If niggers of these days done see what I seed in slavery time they'd pray and thank they Gawd every day. My master's place sot right 'cross the big road from a place they cut and slashed they niggers. You'd hear that white man's black folks bellerin' like cows. I's stood many a time on our front gallery and seed them cut and slash the blood off them niggers. I seed old women half-bent from beatin's goin' to the field. They overseer had a wooden paddle with nails in it. I used to say to missy, 'Why they cuttin' and slashin' them black folks that-a-way?' Missy say, 'Dianah, that there white man got the debbil in him.'

"I seed them sell my mama. I ask my old missy why and she say, 'To go to her husband.'

"When the war broke out I's a full-grown woman. New Orleans was full of sojers and they wouldn't let us go to town. Me and young Mr. Tom used to git on the roof and watch them. The cannons was roarin' like thunder and smoke thick and black as clouds. I got scart when they sot the niggers free, at the niggers shoutin'. I didn't know what 'twas for. Old Miss say to me, 'They been in slavery but you don't know what slavery is, Dianah.'

"Two years after that my old miss carries me to Galveston to my mammy. She tell her to take good care of me and we lived there three years and moved to Jefferson. Our things come by boat but we come in wagons. I married John Smith purty soon after that but he died 'fore long. Then I married Noah Watson and now he's dead. I done raise six chillen but only one am livin' now and that's my younges' gal and I lives with her here.

"I tells the young race iffen they come up like me they wouldn't act so smart. They needs somebody to take the smartness outten them. But my gal am good to me. I gits a pension and pays it to her to take care of me. I been here a hundred years and more and I won't stay much longer, and I don't want to be no 'spense to nobody."

United States. Work Projects Administration

EMMA WATSON

Emma Watson, born in 1852 or 1853, in Ellis Co., Texas, was one of the slaves of the Carl Forrester family. Emma worked in the fields most of her life, but is now too old to work, and is cared for by her daughter. They live at 318 Allen St., Dallas, Texas.

"I axed my old missus when I's borned and she rec'lect I'm eight or nine year old when de freedom war starts. She say she don't make recall de 'xact time, but I takes May for a birthin' time. They's a time when some sich was writ in de Bible, but it got burnt up 'fore I's ageable. I knows where I'm borned, though, and it am on Capt. Forrester's farm in Ellis County. His mother, Miss Susan, raises me like she am my mammy. I calls her Sis Sue. She was old miss and Miss Lee was young miss.

"My paw, I don't know nothin' 'bout. My sister Anna and me, us have de same paw, but my mammy's sold out of Miss'sippi 'way from my paw 'fore my birthin'. My maw kept de name of Lucindy Lane, but Martha and Jennie, my other sisters, had diff'rent paws.

"I's gone through so much of hard times all my life, but when I's de li'l gal I didn't have much to do 'cept tend my Aunt Matilda's babies and wash they clothes. The rest the time I jes' plays round. Miss Lee have a china doll with a wreath of roses round it head. We takes turns playin' with it. I had a rag doll, and it jes' a bundle of rags with strings tied round it to give it a shape. Us make playhouses. Capt. Forrester goes away and I heared he gone to some war, but, law me, I didn't know 'bout war den.

I's jus' glad to play and eat anythin' I can git. When I git a tin can of clabber and some bread, that's what I wanted. They didn't buy no dishes for nigger young'uns to break up. Us et bacon and beef and salt pork and cornbread with us fingers. Mussel shells is what we dipped 'stead of spoons. I did love de souse, too.

"When I had de chills, Sis Sue, dat Old Miss, come out to de quarters and give me sweet milk boiled with pepper. I got shut of dem chills 'cause I didn't like dat pepper tea, but I like it better'n quinine or sage tea. I didn't like to be sick noways, 'cause dey jus' two bedsteads, one for my mammy and my step-paw, and one for us gals.

"They allus promise me they'll larn me to read and write, but never did git to dat. Aunt Matilda did most de spinnin' and weavin' and sewin'. I used to wear a shimmy and a dress in de week and a clean one for Sunday. In winter sometimes us have a li'l sacque and homemake calfskin shoes but mostly us have to stay inside iffen de weather ain't mod'rate.

"De only frolics I 'member was candy pullin's on Christmas. Dat all us niggers knowed 'bout Christmas.

"One day Miss Tilda git de buggy whip to whip my mammy. It's noontime, and dey had blowed de horn for de field niggers to come eat. Maw grabs de whip and says, 'Miss Tilda, you ain't gwine do dat.' Miss Tilda didn't say nothin' for a day or two, den she say, 'Lucindy, you git your young'uns and leave dis place.' So us goes walkin' down de road till us come to some folk's house and dey takes us in. Us dere 'bout a month when mammy git sick. Dem folks sends word to de Forresters dere niggers am sick and Sis Sue hitch up de hoss and come over. She brung food for us every day, and say, 'Now, Lucindy, when you git able you bring your young'uns on home and 'have yourself.' My mammy dies when I's 'bout ten year old.

Emma Watson

"After Capt. Forrester come back home dey tell us to watch out for de Feds. Sis Sue say dey kill nigger young'uns. One day I's comin' through de fields and see three men in blue coats on big bay hosses. I ran, but dey passes me by big as you please. I seed plenty after dat, 'cause dey come and asks for corn and Sis Sue allus say us don't have 'nough for de hosses. But dat night de corn allus leave de cribs. Dem Feds was sho' thievin' folks.

"I stays with de Forresters till I's 22 year old, and dey give me food and clothes, but never no money. Sis Sue used to say, 'Come here, you li'l old free nigger.' It make me so mad. But den I marries and have de swiss white dress and us walk 'cross de fields to de preachers. Dat every bit of fixin' us have.

"Den us raise crops on de half-shares and sot up housekeepin' with a bedstead, some quilts and a li'l old stove. I has four young'uns and every one of dem had schoolin' and larnin'."

JAMES WEST

James West, 83, was born a slave to Mr. William West, near Ripley, in Tippah Co., Mississippi. This was close to the battle fought near Corinth and James witnessed some exciting events. In 1885 James came to Texas and now lives with a friend at 1114 Hardy St., Fort Worth, Texas.

"Yes, suh, I 'members de slavery days and de War, 'cause I's born in 1854, on de plantation of Massa William West, in Mississip'. It weren't a big plantation, jus' 'bout 100 acres, and Massa West owned my mammy and four other slaves, Buck, Sam, Rufus and Mary. I don't know nothin' 'bout my pappy, 'cause I ain't never seed him, and my mammy never told me nothin' of him.

"All us cullud folks lived in cabins and they has two rooms. De bunks is built to de wall and has straw ticks and we has floors and real windows.

"Sam and Buck and Rufus am field workers and plants cotton and sich and looks after de stock. Sometimes de work is heavy and sometimes not. When it am finish, de massa lets 'em go fishin' or visitin' or rest. We goes to church when we wants and we has parties with Sam and Rufus to play de music, de fiddle and de banjo. How I wishes I could be back dere for jus' one year and have it like befo'. Jus' one year befo' I die!

"We has a good massa in every way. Him gives all we can eat. Folks don't eat like we used to, 'cause we had home-cured hams, and when you put it in your mouth, it was a treat for your taster. As for de clothes, massa say, 'De 'terial here and if yous don't supply yourselves, its yous fault.'

"Dere never anyone what gits whippin's on massa's place, 'cept dis nigger, but dey only spankin's. You see, dere was allus a bit of devilment in me. But de massa so good, we all tries to please him and we has no whippin's.

"De massa gives me a he goat and de shoemaker makes me de harness and cart for dat goat and when I gits him trained good, I has a job gittin' de chips for kindlin' and de wood and I totes de water. One day I takes Billy, de goat, 'cross de road for wood and it downhill from de woodpile so I jus' rides de load. Billy was gwine jus' as nice as yous kin like, but him says BAAH, and starts to run like a skeert bull. I thinks what kin be wrong with dat fool goat, when somethin' hits me back of de neck like a coal of fire, and de cart hits a rock and off I goes. To says I's skeert am not tellin' de truf, and I starts hollerin'. It was de bee stung me and when I gits to de house I looks Billy over and, sho' 'nough, on his hip was de bee sting. Dat bee sting sho' put de life in Billy.

"'bout de War time, de plantation was near whar dey fights a battle two days and I seed lots of soldiers. Before dat, de soldiers begins to come to massa's house and water de hosses and eat de lunch. Dey never did raid his place like other places 'round dere, but I hides when dey comes, 'cause I skeert of dem. I quavers and gits skeert when I sees 'em.

"We is jus' settin' down to breakfast one mornin' and we hears a big boomin'. When dat start, dis nigger don't eat his breakfast. I starts for some place to hide. I runs to one place, den I hears de boom, den I runs to another place. I finally crawls under de shed and dere I stays. Dey couldn't git me out and dere I stays for dat day and night and 'til noon de nex' day. I has no water or food. Lots of folks from Ripley what massa knows was kilt in dat battle.

"Buck and I goes to de battleground after de fightin' quits and dere was heaps of dead hosses but dey had dug de trench and buried de dead soldiers.

James West

"I don' know about de Klux, but we use to sing a song 'bout de patter rollers, like dis,

    'Run nigger run, patter roller kotch you,
    Run nigger run, 'cause it almos' day,

> Dat nigger run, dat nigger flew,
> Dat nigger los' his Sunday shoe.'

"I stays with de massa after freedom 'til I's 21 year old and den I leaves and works for diff'runt folks. I marries in Tennessee when I's 22 and we has one chile, but my wife takes him when he's five and leaves, and I never seen or heard of 'em since. I comes to Texas 'bout 52 year ago.

"I has 'joyed talkin' 'bout dem old days, 'cause talk am all I kin do since my legs have de misery so bad."

United States. Work Projects Administration

ADELINE WHITE

Adeline White, 90 odd years old, was born at Opelousas, Louisiana, a slave of Dr. Bridget. She lives with her daughter, Lorena, in Beaumont, Texas.

"I's born at Opelousas and my massa and missis was Dr. Bridget and his wife. They was mean and they beat us and put the hounds after us. They beat the little ones and the big ones and when massa ain't beatin' his wife is. It am continual. My pappy call Thomas Naville and my mammy 'Melia Naville. They was born in Virginia. I had four brothers and two sisters, all dead now.

"Like I says, old massa sho' whip us and when he whip he put us 'cross a barrel or chain us and stake us out with a rope. We didn't have much to eat and not much clothes. They weave us clothes on the loom and make the dress like a sack slip over the head.

"Our cabin wasn't so bad, made of logs with dirt 'tween the logs. The chimney make out of sticks and dirt and some windows with a wooden shutter and no glass in 'em. Massa give 'em lumber and paint to make things for the house and they have homemake bed and table and benches to sit on.

"Massa have the hoss power cotton gin and a hoss power sugar cane mill, too. Us work hard all day in the gin and the sugar cane mill and doesn't have no parties nor fun. Sometimes in the evenin' us git together and talk or sing low, so the white folks won't hear.

Adeline White

"I 'member going through the woods one time and seein' somethin' black come up 'fore me. It must a been a ghost. I got a boy call' Henry what live in Welch and he kin see ghosties all the time. He jus' look back over he lef' shoulder and see plenty of 'em. He say they has a warm heat what make him sweat.

"Old massa didn't go to the war and his boys was too little. We jus' heared about the war and that it was goin' to free us. In the night us would creep out way in the woods and have the prayer meetin', prayin' for freedom to come quick. We has to be careful for if massa find out he whip all of us, sho'. We stays nearly all night and sleeps and prays and sleeps and prays. At las' we hears freedom is on us and massa say we are all free to go, but if we stay he pay us some. Most of us goes, for that massa am sho' mean and if we doesn't have to stay we wouldn't, not with that massa.

"We scatters and I been marry twice. The first man was Eli Evans in Jennings, in Louisiana and us have six chillen. The second man he James White but I has no more chillen. Now I lives with my gal what called Lorena and she make me happy. She sho' good to her old mammy, what ain't much good no more."

SYLVESTER SOSTAN WICKLIFFE

Sylvester Sostan Wickliffe, of Ames, Texas, was born in St. Mary's Parish, Louisiana, in 1854. A free-born Negro, Wickliffe tells an interesting story about his life and that of his uncle, Romaine Vidrine, who was a slave-holder. Wickliffe has a nicely furnished home in Beaumont, and two of his children have been to college.

"I's what dey call a free-born nigger. Its a long story how dat come about, but I can tell you.

"Three Frenchmen come to Louisiana from France. In three generations dey mix with Indians and Negroes. Dey high-born Frenchmen and 'cumulate plenty property. Before dey die dey make 'greement 'mongst demselves. When one die de property go to de other two; de last one livin' git all three plantations and all dat's on dem. It so happen dat old man Vidrine's daddy live longes', so he git it all. But he so good he divide up and my daddy gits forty acres good land. My daddy's greatgrandpapa was one dem first three Frenchmen.

"My daddy was Michael and mama was Lucy and dey a whole passel chillen, Frances, Mary, Clotilde, Astasia and Tom, Samuel, Gilbert and Edward. My daddy was part Indian and I had some half-brothers and sisters what wore blanket and talk Indian talk. Dey used to come see daddy and set round and talk half de night and I never understan' a word dey sayin'.

"Mama didn't have no Indian blood in her, but she born in Louisiana and a right purty, brown-skin woman, probably some French or Spanish in her.

"My uncle, Romaine Vidrine, de son of old man Vidrine, he have de bigges' property. He was a slave-holder. Dey was a number niggers in Louisiana what owned slaves. Romaine, he have 'bout thirty-eight. Dey was a big dif'ence make 'tween slave niggers and owner niggers. Dey so much dif'ence as 'tween white folks and cullud folks. My uncle wouldn't 'low slave niggers to eat at de same table with him or with any of us free-born niggers.

"Folks come down from de noth sometimes and mistook de slave for de owner or de owner for de slave. My uncle was sech a purty, bright man, he must of been a quadroon. He had long burnsides and a long tail coat all de time. He was very dignified. He was good to all he slaves, but when he say work, he mean work. He ain't never 'low none de slaves be familiar with him.

"De old Romaine house was a old*fashioned house make out of cypress. Dat everlastin'. It come to a peak on top and dere was one big room what run de whole length in de back and dat de sleepin' room for all de li'l chillen. De growed-up folks have sleepin' rooms, too. Dey have a cook shack outside. It a sep'rate house.

"Us live in a purty good house not very far from de big house. Dey have what dey calls a private school. It was kep' by my uncle. Only de free-born niggers went to it.

De older ones educated in French and de young ones in French and 'merican, too. After de war dey hire a white man named William Devoe to be teacher. He educate de chillen to de third gen'ration. He come to Texas with me and die 'bout five years ago.

"When a couple want to git marry on de old Romaine place, uncle sent for de priest from St. Martin. Dey wasn't no priest round Franklin or what dey call New Iberia later. When I's most a growed boy de priest come baptise 'bout forty of us. He use de water* out uncle's cistern for de ceremony. When us goin' down de road to de baptisin' dey's a squirrel run 'cross de road and us chillen all broke and run to cotch it. Law, dat jus' 'bout scare my old godmother to death. She took so much pain dat us all nice and clean and 'fraid us git dirty. Her name was Nana Ramon Boutet and she live here in Ames settlement for many year. Us laugh many time 'bout dat squirrel.

"Dey used to call us de free Mulattoes from 'cross de bayou. De nearest town was Pattersonville and it five mile away. Now dey calls de settlement Vidrinville for old man Romaine Vidrine. De plantation suppor' a grist mill and a raw sugar mill. Dey make de sugar dark, big grain, 'cause dey ain't no 'finery in dem days. Dey put de sugar in big five hunerd pound hogshead and take it by boat down de Teche to New Orleans and sell it. Dey use de money to buy coffee and cotton. Us didn't raise cotton. I never see no cotton till I's a big boy and come to Fort LaFayette.

"De grist mill was built 'way from de house. Dey have a long lever what stand out de side and hitch hosses with a rawhide belt to make de mill turn. Us folks all raise rice. Not like now, Lawdy, no. Dey jes' plant rice in rows like corn and cultivate it like any other crop. Dey wasn't no irrigation ditch. After de rice harves' dey put it in a mortar make out a cypress log or block and knock de roughness off de rice with de pestle.

"Every fall us go huntin' deer round Chicimachi Lake. Dey calls it Grand Lake now, but de reg'lar Indian name am Chicimachi. Dere was a tribe of Indians by dat name. Dey wasn't copper skin, but more yaller like.

"When war commence it purty hard on folks. Us see soldiers comin' 'cross de bayou in blue suits. Dey raid de sugar mill and take de livestock and foodstuff on de Pumphrey place. Dey have a awful battle five mile away. Dat at Camp Boesland, on de Teche. Dat a awful battle! My brother go dere next day and see soldiers standin' up dead 'gainst trees with dey bay'nets still sot.

"De Confed'rates come and took all de slaves to build de fort at Alexandria. When dey come to de Romaine place dey see niggers, and ain't know which free and which slaves. Dey line my daddy up with de others, but a white man from town say, 'Dat a good, old man. He part Indian and he free. He a good citizen. He ain't s'pose do work like dat.' So dey didn't take him.

"De Yankees damage de Romaine property 'siderable. Dey take a whole year crop of sugar and corn and hosses. Afterwards dey pass a law and de gov'ment 'low money for dat. It was 'bout twenty year before dey git de' money, but dey git it. Romaine and he heirs git $30,000 for dem damages.

"After war over, old man Romaine tell he slaves dey free now. But he say, 'You is most born right here and iffen you is bright you stay right here.' Dey all did stay.

But dey ain't never git to jine with de free-born. Dey still make a dif'ence.

"After freedom I 'cide to larn a trade. I 'prentice myself to de blacksmith trade for clothes and board. I larn all I can in three year and quit and open a shop on Bayou Tortue, 'tween St. Martin and Lafayette. I charge $2.00 for to shoe a hoss all de way round. Den I beat plows, build two-wheel buggy and hack. I make sweepstocks and Garrett and Cottman plow. Dat after de time of de wood mould boards. I make mine with metal.

"I come to Texas in 1890, to Liberty, and been right round dere and Ame for forty-seven year. I start me a gin and blacksmith shop when I first come. I marry in Houston to Epheme Pradia, 'nother free-born nigger, and I still marry to her after forty-seven year. Dat a good long hitch. We have seven chillen, all livin'. One gal went to de Catholic church school in Galveston. One boy go to Pradeau University in New Orleans. Dey two blacksmith, one farmer, one good auto mechanic and de three gals keeps house.

"I 'member lots of songs us sing in French but I can't give 'merican for dem. I know de song, *LaLoup Garou*. I try to translate one song for you:

> "Master of de house
> Give me meat without salt;
> When de stranger come,
> He give me roast chicken."

United States. Work Projects Administration

DAPHNE WILLIAMS

Daphne Williams was born in Tallahassee, Florida, a slave to Mrs. Nancy Herring. Daphne does not know her exact age, but must be close to or over 100. She claims to have witnessed the fall of the stars in 1833. She lives in Beaumont, Texas.

"It won't be long 'fore I's sleeping the long sleep. I expect I's about the mos' agreeables person in the county, 'cause I's so old. I's born in Tallahassee, in Florida, but I don' know when. The Herrings used to own me and I took their name. Missus' name was Nancy Herring and the marster was still alive when I's born, but he die when I's a baby. I guess I's about 10 or 12 year old when us come to Texas.

"Dat place where I's born was sho' a place! They have a three-story house with a porch at the front and another at the back. They was posties what stand from one porch floor to the nex' and brace it up. I used to live in the big house, 'cause I's nuss for the white chillen. I didn' stay round with cullud folks a-tall.

"The missus was a widow woman ever since I 'member her. She have two boy and three gal, and that sho' was a lovely house. They have they ownself painted in pictures on the wall, jus' as big as they is. They have them in big frames like gold. And they have big mirrors from the floor to the ceilin'. You could see you ownself walk in them.

"My mother was named Millie and my daddy named Daniel. I don' know how many niggers missus have on the plantation. I was never 'lowed to play with the cullud chillen, but I have two brothers named Abram and Handy and I seed them sometimes. I took care of the white chillen and took 'em to church. Iffen baby git to cryin' I walked round with him, but you better be careful not to let the briar scratch him or he git a scar on him and then they gwinter put a scar on you.

"They give me pretty clothes to wear and make me keep clean and expectable. I wore homespun and gingham dresses, jus' cut straight down. They didn' have no sewin' 'chine. They have a woman to cut out and sew and she do that all day long.

"My white folks have mighty nice company. My missus up on the top. They have nice, fine, intelligen' dishes and table cloth.

"They give us holiday on Christmas and sometimes a whole week. They treat the white chillen and black chillen all good and give 'em whippin' iffen they needs it. When there's disturbance, missus holler, 'You all chillen, come in here to me,' and whip us all, then she know she whip the right one.

"I seed the stars fall. God give me a good eyesight. The sun was shinin' and it was plain daylight and the stars fall jus' like hail, only they never fall all the way to the groun'. They fall so far and then they stop and go out. They stay up in the element all the time. Missus sent for the niggers to come up to the house and pray. All that time the stars was a-comin' through the element. All the darkies, little and big, was a-prayin' on their knees, 'cause they thing the jedgment sho' come then.

"Before us move from Florida us git mos' us goods for clothes from North and South Carolina. The war commence in North Caroline to the good of my recollection. That was six month or a year after us lef' Florida. They was a-tryin' to smuggle it down then. When the missus 'cided come to Texas she sent the niggers on ahead and they done make two crops 'fore us git there. The place was five mile from Woodville. We come to Texas in a boat what's big as a house. When the boat git there I was so 'cited when I seed all the pretty trees. I never mever used to trees, 'cause from where us come was jus' prairie land far's you kin see. No tree round Tallahassee and no hill.

"My mother was cook and when she like to die one time they starts breakin' me in to do the cookin'. Then when she die I was cook and been doing that two, three year when freedom come.

Daphne Williams

"When they tol' us freedom come us thought they was foolin'. My uncle say we's free and to go and look out for number one. They let us stay awhile, but they 'lowanced us. Iffen us spen' the 'lowance us jus' had to go rustle up something to eat or do without. My daddy was a widow man by then and he stay, 'cause he say he want to see further into the subjec'.

"One time I gwineter see my father and had my baby in my arms, 'cause I done married. I was gwine through the wilderness and I heared something squall like a woman cry. I 'gin walk faster. The squall come again. Something say to me, 'You better run.' The hair commence stand on my head and I walk pretty peart. That squall come again and I run fastes' I knows how. I have that poor little baby carried any way.

When I get to the fence I jump over and sot down. The chillen come running and say, 'Yonder Daphne.' They help me into the house but I's so scart I couldn' tell 'em till near bedtime and then I say I hear squall like woman cryin'. Mister Goolsbee say, 'Daphne, make soun' like you hear,' and I makes a squall, and he say, 'That a panther and iffen he kotched you that would have been the end of you and that baby of yourn what you was totin'.' So 'bout four o' clock in that mornin' he gits 'bout fourteen neighbors and the dawgs and they hunts that rascal and runs him in 'bout 8 or 10 o'clock. A span of mules couldn' pull that rascal, I don' 'lieve. He have the biggest tushes I ever seed with these two eyes. They put him in a pot and bile him and make soap out of the grease. That panther didn' git me or my baby but they got him and made soap out of him."

HORATIO W. WILLIAMS

Horatio W. Williams, known as "Rash" to his friends, is 83 years old. He was a slave of Woodruff Norseworthy, in Pine Bluff, Arkansas. Horatio has lived in Jasper, Texas, for many years.

"I was born in slavery in Pine Bluff in de state of Arkansas, on July 2, 1854, and dey tells me dat make me 'bout 84 years old. Woodruff Norseworthy was my owner and boss all de time I a slave. I marry in 1875 and I lost my wife two year ago, and when a man looses a good woman he loses somethin'. Us had 13 chillen, but only two of dem alive now.

"My boss man was mean to he niggers and I 'member crawlin' down through de woods and listenin' one time when he beat a nigger. Every time he hit him he pray. Boss have 15 slaves and I recollect one time he gwine beat my mother. She run to de kitchen and jump behin' de door and cover herself up in de big pile of dirty clothes. Dey never think to look for her there and she stay there all day. But de next day dey cotch her and whip her.

"Dem what runs away, dey gits bloodhounds after 'em. Dey clumb de tree when dey heered dem hounds comin' but de massa make dem git down and dey shoot dem, iffen dey didn't. When dey gits down de dogs jumps all over dem and would tear dem to pieces, but de massa beats dem off.

"Once de boss has company and one our niggers sleeps on de porch outside de company's room, and in de night he slip in dat room and thiefed de fine, white shirt out de suitcase and wears it round de next mornin'.

"Course he couldn't read and he ain't know de [HW: white] man have he name on dat shirt. When de boss find it out he takes dat nigger down in de bottom and I crawls through de bresh and watches. Dey tie he foots together over de limb and let he head hang down and beat him till de blood run down on de roots of dat tree. When dey takes him down he back look like raw meat and he nearly die.

"Sometime when de nigger won't mind dey puts de chain to one foot and a ball on it 'bout big as a nigger's head, and he have to drag it down with him whe ever he go.

"My white folks moved to Bastrop in Louisiana and den to Texas and brung me with them. When us work in de field us have de cook what put us food on big trays and carry it to de field, den we stop and eat it under shade of a tree, if dey any. Dey give us bread and meat and syrup for dinner and us has bacon long as it lasts.

"When I's free I rents land and crops 'round, after I gits marry. Befo' dat, I was here, dere and yonder, for my board and clothes and four bits de day. I give all my chillen de eddication, leastwise dey all kin read and write and dat's what I cain't do.

"I 'longs to de Meth'dist church and I don't unndestan' some dese other churches very well. Seems strange to me dat at dis late time dey's tryin' find new ways of gittin' to Heaven."

United States. Work Projects Administration

LOU WILLIAMS

Lou Williams, said to be the oldest citizen of San Angelo, Texas, was born in southern Maryland in 1829. She and her family were slaves of Abram and Kitty Williams, of that section, and Lou served as nursemaid to her master's children from the age of eight until after the Civil War. She then went to Louisiana where she worked as a cook for several years before coming to San Angelo. She is very active for her 108 years and is a familiar figure about town, with her crutch.

"I's have de bes' white folks in Maryland. I's born in a three-room frame house and I had one of them statements (birth certificates). When I five years old my old missy she say, 'Dat gal, she sho' am gwine be dependable and I makes nursemaid out of her.' When I eight years old she trusts me with dem white chillen. I loves to fish so well I'd take de li'l chillen to de creek and take off my underskirt and spread it out on de bank and put de chillen on it while I sho' cotch de fish. Massa, he start lookin' for me and when he gits to de creek, he say, 'Dar's de li'l devil.' He know dem chillen safe, so he jus' laugh.

"In de fall massa puts us nigger chillen on de bale of cotton and takes us to town and gives us money to buy candy and dolls with. We allus had good food and lots of fish and rabbits and possums, but when my missy see dem possums carryin' de baby possums round she fall out with possum and she say, 'No more possum bein' cooked 'round here.'

"When I jes' a li'l gal I seed de stars fall and when everything got dark like and dem bright stars begin to fall we all start runnin' and hollerin' to our missy and she say, 'Chillen, don't git under my coat, git on your knees and start prayin', and when we begins to pray de Lawd he sends a shower of rain and puts out dem stars or de whole world would a been burned up.

"When massa take us to town he say he want us to see how de mean slave owners raffles off de fathers and de husban's and de mothers and de wives and de chillen. He takes us 'round to de big platform and a white man git up dere with de slave and start hollerin' for bids, and de slave stands dere jes' pitiful like, and when somebody buy de slave all de folks starts yellin' and a cryin'. Dem sho' was bad times. Our massa wouldn't do his niggers dat way and we loved him for it, too.

"We had big gardens and lots of vegetables to eat, 'cause massa had 'bout eight hundred slaves and 'bout a thousand acres in he plantation. In summer time we wore jes' straight cotton slips and no shoes till Sunday, den we puts on shoes and white dresses and ties a ribbon 'round our waists, and we didn't look like de same chillen.

"Dere a big arbor for de whites to go to church and we goes, too. When we starts down de road to church, our mama, she start sayin' things to make us be quiet. We pass de graveyard and she say, 'See dat spirit runnin' 'long here with us?' When we gits dere we hardly moves. We could jine, if we wants to.

"My mama, she Black Creek Indian and none of dem white folks wants her. When massa buys my daddy and us chillen we had done been sold 'way from her and we cry and she cry, and den she follow us to our plantation and cry and beg our massa let her stay. He say, 'She ain't no good but put her in de house and let her do some patchin' and mendin'.' Mama, she cry and say, 'Thank God, Thank God! I's git to be with my husban' and li'l chillen.' She make de good spinner and weaver and old missy, she say she couldn't do without her, 'cause she spin cotton cloth for summer and woolen cloth for winter.

"Niggers didn't have much weddin's, but when massa find dem takin' up he tells everybody to dress in white and de two what was takin' up together has to march up and down till de big supper comes off. Dey was man and wife den, but me, I's diff'rent. I's had a 'spectable weddin', 'cause missy, she say I's her nursemaid. De preacher, he reads, and I's all dressed in white clothes and sech a supper we never had befo'.

"All de slaves wasn't so lucky as we was, though. We lives close to de meanest owner in de country. Our massa wouldn't keep no overseer, 'cause he say his niggers wasn't dogs, but dis other man he keeps overseers to beat de niggers and he has de big leather bullwhip with lead in de end, and he beats some slaves to death. We heared dem holler and holler till dey couldn't holler no mo'! Den dey jes' sorta grunt every lick till dey die. We finds big streams of blood where he has whopped dem and when it rained de whole top of de ground jes' looks like a river of blood dere. Sometime he bury he niggers and sometime de law come out and make him bury dem. He put dem in chains and stockades and sometimes he would buck and gag dem.

Lou Williams

"We seed he niggers goin' by our plantation with de oven on de heads 'round three o'clock in de mornin' on de way to de fields. Dese ovens made of wood and tin over de tin cup dat fit de slaves' heads. Each nigger have he bread and some old hairy bone meat a-cookin' with fire coals in dese ovens. Dey made not to burn de head and when dey gits to de fields dey sets dem down to finish cookin' while dey works till breakfast time. De mamas what expectin' babies was whopped to make dem work faster and when babies was sick dey has to put dem in de basket on top dere heads and take dem to de cotton patch, and put dem under de cotton stalks and try to 'tend to dem. Lawd, Lawd, dem was awful times, and I sho' is glad I has good white folks.

Lou Williams' House

"Some dat man's niggers allus runnin' 'way and dey sets de nigger dogs on dem and catch dem mos' times. Den dey treat 'em so bad dey wouldn't never want to run away no more.

"We allus gits Saturday evenin' off to wash our clothes and sometime we has dances Saturday night. I has two brothers, Jim and William and William git kilt in de war. My two sisters named Relia and Laura. We has corn shuckin's and big suppers and on Christmas our massa buys us de present, most times shoes, 'cause we didn't have any shoes.

"When de white folks dies or gits married everybody sho' carries on big. When we sick dey gives us snakeroot tea and cana and sage tea and if we's bad sick, dey gits de doctor. Missy, she make hog hoof tea, jes' bile de hoofs in good whiskey for de cold. Den she put camphor ball and asafoetida 'round our necks to keep off diseases.

"When de war ends we sees a white man comin' down de road on a hoss and de road full of niggers followin' him, singin' and shoutin' and prayin'. I stays with massa till he die, then I marries and has one chile and one grandchile, and I lives with her."

MILLIE WILLIAMS

Millie Williams, 86, lives at 1612 E. Fourth St., Fort Worth, Texas. She was born a slave to Joe Benford, in Tennessee, was sold to Bill Dunn, who brought her to Texas and traded her to Tommy Ellis for some land. She has lived in Fort Worth since the 1870's.

"I don't know when I was born, 'cause I was taken from my folks when I was a baby, but massa told me I was born in de spring of de year, in 1851. I know I been in dis world a long time, but I has have good white folks. I was born on Massa Benford's place in Tennessee and my mama's name was Martha Birdon. She say my pappy's name Milton Wade, but I never seed him. And I didn't know my mama a long time, 'cause she's sold away from Massa Benford's place, and I was sold with her, den he took me back, and I never seed my mama no mo'.

"After I was sold back to Massa Benford, he puts me in de nigger yard. Dat whar de massa kep' slaves what he traded. It was jus' a bunch of shacks throwed together and dirty was no name for it, it was worse than a pig pen. De man what watch over us in dat nigger yard was de meanest man what ever lived. He'd take a club and beat de daylight out of us, 'cause de club wouldn't leave scars like de bullwhip, and didn't bring de price down when we is sold.

"One day Massa Benford takes us to town and puts us on dat auction block and a man name Bill Dunn bought me. I was 'bout seven years old. Talkin' 'bout somethin' awful, you should have been dere. De slave owners was shoutin' and sellin' chillen to one man and de mama and pappy to 'nother. De slaves cries and takes on somethin' awful. If a woman had lots of chillen she was sold for mo', 'cause it a sign she a good breeder.

"Right after I was sold to Massa Dunn, dere was a big up-risin' in Tennessee and it was 'bout de Union, but I don't know what it was all about, but dey wanted Massa Dunn to take some kind of a oath, and he wouldn't do it and he had to leave Tennessee. He said dey would take de slaves 'way from him, so he brought me and Sallie Armstrong to Texas. Dere he trades us to Tommy Ellis for some land and dat Massa Ellis, he de best white man what ever lived. He was so good to us we was better off dan when we's free.

"Massa Ellis' plantation was one of de bigges', and he owned land as far as we could see. Dere was 'bout 50 slaves and we lived in a row of log cabins long side de big house. In winter we sleeps inside but in summer we sleeps in de yard, and de same 'bout eatin'. Sometimes massa fed good and den 'gain he didn't, but dat 'cause of de War. We has cornbread and milk and all de coffee you would drink. On Sundays we fills de pot half full of meat and shell peas on top de meat.

"I 'member de time we steals one of massa's big chickens and its in de pot in de fireplace when we seed missy comin'. I grabs dat chicken and pot and puts it under de bed and puts de bedclothes top dat pot. Missy, she come in and say, 'I sho' do smell somethin' good.' I say,

'Whar, Missy Ellis?' She don't find nothin' so she leaves. When she's gone I takes dat chicken and we eats it in a hurry.

"De overseer woke 'em up 'bout four in de mornin', but I works in de house. De field workers gits off Thursdays and Saturday evenin's and Sunday. De reason dey gits off Thursday is dat de massa has some kind of thought we shouldn't work dat day. Maybe it was 'ligion, I don't know.

"We has parties and sings

'Massa sleeps in de feather bed,
Nigger sleeps on de floor;
When we'uns gits to Heaven,
Dey'll be no slaves no mo'.'

"Den we has de song 'bout dis:

'Rabbit in de briar patch,
Squirrel in de tree,
Wish I could go huntin',
But I ain't free.
'Rooster's in de henhouse,
Hen's in de patch,
Love to go shootin',
But I ain't free.'

"When de nigger leaves de plantation without no pass, and de padder rollers kotched him, dey gives him 39 licks with de bullwhip. When we's in de fields and sees de padder roller ride by, we starts murmerin' out loud, 'Patter de pat, patter de pat.' One after 'nother took it up and purty soon everybody murmerin'. We allus do dat to let everybody know de padder roller 'round. Den we sing songs 'bout 'em, too.

Millie Williams

"When War start dere a army camp jus' below de plantation, and 'bout a thousand soldiers. We hears 'em shout, 'Halt, march, halt, march,' all day long. Dey sung 'Lincoln's not satisfied,

> He wants to fight 'gain,
> All he got to do,
> Is hustle up his men.'

"I stays with Massa Ellis after we's freed. Dere sho' was a mighty purty sight when de slaves knows dey's free. Dey hug one 'nother and almos' tear dere clothes off. Some cryin' for de husban', and some cryin' for de chillen.

"When I was 'bout 20 I lef' massa's home and moves to Dallas, whar I marries my first man. His name was Bill Jackson. He lef' me and goes back to Dallas and I hear he die, so I marry Will Williams and he dies. Now I been here since de Lawd know when."

United States. Work Projects Administration

ROSE WILLIAMS

Rose Williams is over 90. She was owned by William Black, a trader whose plantation lay in Bell County, Texas. Rose and her parents were sold in 1860 to Hall Hawkins, of Bell County. Rose was forced to mate with a slave named Rufus when she was about sixteen, and had two children by him, one born after Rose was freed. She forced Rufus to leave her and never married. For the last ten years Rose has been blind. She lives at 1126 Hampton St., Fort Worth, Texas.

"What I say am de facts. If I's one day old, I's way over 90, and I's born in Bell County, right here in Texas, and am owned by Massa William Black. He owns mammy and pappy, too. Massa Black has a big plantation but he has more niggers dan he need for work on dat place, 'cause he am a nigger trader. He trade and buy and sell all de time.

"Massa Black am awful cruel and he whip de cullud folks and works 'em hard and feed dem poorly. We'uns have for rations de cornmeal and milk and 'lasses and some beans and peas and meat once a week. We'uns have to work in de field every day from daylight till dark and on Sunday we'uns do us washin'. Church? Shucks, we'uns don't know what dat mean.

"I has de correct mem'randum of when de war start.

Massa Black sold we'uns right den. Mammy and pappy powerful glad to git sold, and dey and I is put on de block with 'bout ten other niggers. When we'uns gits to de tradin' block, dere lots of white folks dere what came to look us over. One man shows de intres' in pappy. Him named Hawkins. He talk to pappy and pappy talk to him and say, 'Dem my woman and chiles. Please buy all of us and have mercy on we'uns.' Massa Hawkins say, 'Dat gal am a likely lookin' nigger, she am portly and strong, but three am more dan I wants, I guesses.'

"De sale start and 'fore long pappy am put on de block. Massa Hawkins wins de bid for pappy and when mammy am put on de block, he wins de bid for her. Den dere am three or four other niggers sold befo' my time comes. Den massa Black calls me to de block and de auction man say, 'What am I offer for dis portly, strong young wench. She's never been 'bused and will make de good breeder.'

"I wants to hear Massa Hawkins bid, but him say nothin'. Two other men am biddin' 'gainst each other and I sho' has de worryment. Dere am tears comin' down my cheeks 'cause I's bein' sold to some man dat would make sep'ration from my mammy. One man bids $500 and de auction man ask, 'Do I hear more? She am gwine at $500.00.' Den someone say, $525.00 and de auction man say, 'She am sold for $525.00 to Massa Hawkins.' Am I glad and 'cited! Why, I's quiverin' all over.

"Massa Hawkins takes we'uns to his place and it am a nice plantation. Lots better am dat place dan Massa Black's. Dere is 'bout 50 niggers what is growed and lots of chillen. De first thing massa do when we'uns gits home am give we'uns rations and a cabin. You mus' believe dis nigger when I says dem rations a feast for us. Dere plenty meat and tea and coffee and white flour. I's never tasted white flour and coffee and mammy fix some biscuits and coffee. Well, de biscuits was yum, yum, yum to me, but de coffee I doesn't like.

"De quarters am purty good. Dere am twelve cabins all made from logs and a table and some benches and bunks for sleepin' and a fireplace for cookin' and de heat. Dere am no floor, jus' de ground.

"Massa Hawkins am good to he niggers and not force 'em work too hard. Dere am as much diff'ence 'tween him and old Massa Black in de way of treatment as 'twixt de Lawd and de devil. Massa Hawkins 'lows he niggers have reason'ble parties and go fishin', but we'uns am never tooken to church and has no books for larnin'. Dare am no edumcation for de niggers.

"Dere am one thing Massa Hawkins does to me what I can't shunt from my mind. I knows he don't do it for meanness, but I allus holds it 'gainst him. What he done am force me to live with dat nigger, Rufus, 'gainst my wants.

"After I been at he place 'bout a year, de massa come to me and say, 'You gwine live with Rufus in dat cabin over yonder. Go fix it for livin'.' I's 'bout sixteen year old and has no larnin', and I's jus' igno'mus chile. I's thought dat him mean for me to tend de cabin for Rufus and some other niggers. Well, dat am start de pestigation for me.

"I's took charge of de cabin after work am done and fixes supper. Now, I don't like dat Rufus, 'cause he a bully. He am big and 'cause he so, he think everybody do what him say. We'uns has supper, den I goes here and dere talkin', till I's ready for sleep and den I gits in de bunk. After I's in, dat nigger come and crawl in de bunk with me 'fore I knows it. I says, 'What you means, you fool nigger?' He say fer me to hush de mouth. 'Dis am my bunk, too,' he say.

"You's teched in de head. Git out,' I's told him, and I puts de feet 'gainst him and give him a shove and out he go on de floor 'fore he know what I's doin'. Dat nigger jump up and he mad. He look like de wild bear. He starts for de bunk and I jumps quick for de poker. It am 'bout three foot long and when he comes at me I lets him have it over de head. Did dat nigger stop in he tracks? I's say he did. He looks at me steady for a minute and you's could tell he thinkin' hard. Den he go and set on de bench and say, 'Jus wait. You thinks it am smart, but you's am foolish in de head. Dey's gwine larn you somethin'.

"'Hush yous big mouth and stay 'way from dis nigger, dat all I wants,' I say, and jus' sets and hold dat poker in de hand. He jus' sets, lookin' like de bull. Dere we'uns sets and sets for 'bout an hour and den he go out and I bars de door.

"De nex' day I goes to de missy and tells her what Rufus wants and missy say dat am de massa's wishes. She say, 'Yous am de portly gal and Rufus em de portly man. De massa wants you-uns for to bring forth portly chillen.

"I's thinkin' 'bout what de missy say, but say to myse'f, 'I's not gwine live with dat Rufus.' Dat night when him come in de cabin, I grabs de poker and sits on de bench and says, 'Git 'way from me, nigger, 'fore I busts yous brains out and stomp on dem.' He say nothin' and git out.

"De nex' day de massa call me and tell me, 'Woman, I's pay big money for you and I's done dat for de cause I wants yous to raise me chillens. I's put yous to live with Rufus for dat purpose. Now, if you doesn't want whippin' at de stake, yous do what I wants.'

"I thinks 'bout massa buyin' me offen de block and savin' me from bein' sep'rated from my folks and 'bout bein' whipped at de stake. Dere it am. What am I's to do? So I 'cides to do as de massa wish and so I yields.

"When we'uns am given freedom, Massa Hawkins tells us we can stay and work for wages or share crop de land. Some stays and some goes. My folks and me stays. We works de land on shares for three years, den moved to other land near by. I stays with my folks till they dies.

"If my mem'randum am correct, it am 'bout thirty year since I come to Fort Worth. Here I cooks for white folks till I goes blind 'bout ten year ago.

"I never marries, 'cause one 'sperience am 'nough for dis nigger. After what I does for de massa, I's never wants no truck with any man. De Lawd forgive dis cullud woman, but he have to 'scuse me and look for some others for to 'plenish de earth."

STEVE WILLIAMS

Steve Williams was born a slave of the Bennett family in 1855. They were residents of Goliad County, Texas and owners of only a small bunch of slaves. He and the other slaves were driven away hurriedly after the soldiers had threatened the slave owners for not having turned the slaves loose as soon after emancipation as they should have. Steve worked around his old home for his victuals and clothes a few years, then drifted about the country as a farm hand, finally landing in San Angelo, Texas where he worked for awhile as cook at a barbecue stand. He now lives alone in the back yard of his niece and is hardly able to get in and out of his small cabin on his crutches.

Steve relates the story of his life as follows:

"I wasn't very big when I was a slave. Fact is, we was set free 'fore I was big enough to remember much about how dey does but I's hear my mother tells 'bout dem Louisiana slave holders, dem what had dem drivers. Now dey was sho' rough on dem. My mother's name was Charlotte Williams and my father he was name Bill and dey belong to de Williams dere, you see, and was sold to Mr. Bennett and brought to Goliad. Dats how come I's named Williams and my marster named Bennett. Our little log huts was put up 'round in de back yard and our beds was home-made, jes' kind of plank scaffolds like. Our beddin' wasn't too good, jes' fair cotton beds. Ole marster's folks dey have big feather beds and a nice log house.

"I never seen any money when I was a boy to 'mount to anything and for a long time after dat war I never seen too much.

"We had pretty good to eat such as vegetables from de boss's garden and plenty of all kinds of meats. Some of de colored folks likes 'possum de best but I always likes coon. Jes' bile him, den bake him good and brown and aint no 'possum can come up wid dat.

"We had good homespun clothes and some times we have shoes.

"I never did see none of the slaves sold but I hear my mother tells 'bout how horrible dat was. I didn' learn much readin' and writin' 'cause no body never teach me none.

"We goes to camp meetin' after de war but not much, den dat was de white folks meetin'.

"On Christmas we usually have a shoat and cakes and lots of fiddlin' and dancin'.

Steve Williams

"Slaves didn' have no weddin's. De boss he jes' puts dem in a cabin and gives dem a wife and dey all calls dat married. Fact is, dey jes' wasn' so much marryin' done 'mong de colored.

"When we hear we was free we hear it from some of de other slaves and we was held longer den some in de north, but one day our boss comes from town and he say to his wife, he say, 'Dem soldiers say iffen we don't git dem niggers 'way from here dey goin' come out here and sweeps us out of de cradle.'

"He sho' got busy den. He comes out and he say, 'You all git, I mean git from here'. So we jes' scatters 'round, here and yonder, not knowin' 'zactly what to do. Some of us works on one farm and some on another for a little co'n or some clothes or food. Finally I works 'round 'til I comes to San Angelo, Texas and I cooks barbecue for a long time 'til I jes' finally breaks down. Now, I don' try to do nothin' but jes' hobble 'round a little on my ole crutches."

WAYMAN WILLIAMS

Wayman Williams does not know his age, but he was a small boy when the slaves were freed. He was born in Mississippi, but the first place he remembers is the Sanama plantation on the Trinity river, in Texas. He now lives on North Falls St., in Mart, Texas.

"I was one of four chillen of Calvin and Julia Williams, of de state of Mississippi, when they was first married, 'fore they come to Texas. But de earlies' 'lection I has, was livin' on a plantation belongin' to a Mr, Sanama. It was on de Trinity river, right down in de bottoms. My folks stayed on dere after freedom and I lived with dem till I was nearly growed. Dere massa give dem supplies and let dem work a piece of land and they give him half de crop.

"I 'member times us go huntin' and kill most anything we want, wild turkeys and wild hawgs and deer. My father used to go out and kill deer and not git out of sight of de house. Livin' was easier den now, for we had all dem things without havin' to buy dem. I 'member de bear hunts. We had great big, brindle dogs for de bears and dey surroun' him and stand him at bay till de men came and kill him.

"A man by name of Burton lived near us, and one day he sent one he boys to town on a little race hoss. On de way home dat boy crossin' de river bottom and a panther git after him, and he race he hoss and outrun dat panther. He jump off de hoss and run in de house and lock de door. De panther try to git in and de men in de field hear he cries and shoots him. In dose days de men took guns to de fields.

"They cotched wolves and bears in traps but de panther was de most dang'rous animal us have to fight. Us never know when he goin' to strike. One our neighbors go to town after a turkey and on he way home a panther was sittin' in a tree by de road, and he make a lunge at de man and grab de turkey and tear de man's arm. Once my grandpa ridin' 'long one night, crossin' de river, and a panther git after him. He had a fast hoss and outran dat panther, and got to de house, and two our bear dogs kep' it off till he shot it. I knows dese things am true, for they happen jes' like I tell it.

"Our house was close to de boat landin' on de river and my father helped unload supplies from de boats, when he not workin' in de fields. Jedge Beavers own de storehouse what kep' de supplies, and he ship he cotton by boat to de Gulf, mostly to Galveston.

"De 'Federate sojers pass our house and go to Jedge for him to give dem something to eat and he allus did. Sometimes dey was men on hosses and he give dem feed for de hosses. Once a crowd young fellows comin' home from de war on hosses and dey got supplies, and de Jedge give dem a little toddy for to make dem feel good. Dey feels so good dey gits some ribbon from de store and tie it to de hosses heads and rides off, with dat ribbon jes' a-streamin' from de hosses mane.

"De Jedge enjoy all day. He felt like dey been fightin' for him and dey welcome to what he have. It was de common thing for de sojers to stop at the house and ask for food or to sleep. Sometimes niggers come, what run away to de North 'fore freedom. Dey done got tired of dat cold weather up dere and when freedom come, dey ready to come back home.

"When de slaves sot free, dey have big times, and feel like dey not work at all. But when old massa give dem a place to farm and tell dem iffen dey don't work dey won't eat, dey stays with him and works de crops on halves, mostly. De nigger do de work and massa feed him and give him team and tools, den massa git half de crop.

"De slaves what went up North and come back, tell how dey call 'Contrabands' up dere. Dey didn't know what it mean, but dey come back anyway.

"Some white school teachers from up North come to teach de chillen, but dey didn't talk like folks here and didn't understan' our talk. Dey didn't know what us mean when us say 'titty' for sister, and 'budder' for brother, and 'nanny' for mammy. Jes' for fun us call ourselves big names to de teacher, some be named General Lee and some Stonewall Jackson. We be one name one day and 'nother name next day. Until she git to know us she couldn't tell de diff'rence, 'cause us all look alike to her. Us have good times tellin' her 'bout black magic and de conjure. Us tell her night birds full of magic and dere feathers roast in ashes work spells what kill evil conjure. If a rabbit run 'cross de path, turn your hat round and wear it hind part befo' to keep bad luck away. A buzzard's claw tie round de baby's neck make teethin' easy. De teacher from de North don't know what to think of all dat. But our old missy, who live here all de time, know all 'bout it. She lets us believe our magic and conjure, 'cause she partly believe it, too.

"I lives in dat place till I's a big boy and den works for Mr. John Mergersen and a Mr. Porter. Dey come from Mississippi right after freedom and was jes' like homefolks. So I works for dem till I gits married and starts out for myself.

"I 'member some songs my mammy and old missy larnt me. One go like dis:

> "'De top bolls ain' open,
> De bottom bolls am rotten.
> I can't git my number here,
> I has to quit and go 'way.
>
> "'When de sun go down and de moon go up,
> Iffen I can't git my number, I can't git my pay.'

"When I was little, my father split de rails out of trees to make fences, and I have an aunt what was de big woman, and she holp. She have a song what go like dis, and when she sing, she come down on a rail, 'biff'.

> "'Times are gittin' hard,' (biff)
> Money's gittin scarce,' (biff)
> Times don't git no better here,' (biff)
> I bound to leave dis place.'

"But when de big meetin' goin' on, dis one de songs dey likes to sing:

> "'As I went down in de valley to pray,
> I met de debbil on my way,
> What you reckon he say to me?

You're too young to die,
And too young to pray,
I made him a lie, and kep' on my way.'

"We raised corn and cotton and potatoes and lots of vegetables and fruit. We didn't have no wheat, so we couldn't have flour and it too high to buy. All dem what could buy it, was de landowner.

"When de corn gathered, us pile it in piles and have corn shuckin' at night, cook our supper and all eat together and listen to de stories tell by de old folks. When dey git de piles of corn ready for shuckin', dey lay a rail in de middle and 'vide de piles, and de side what git through first git supper first. De song go like dis:

"'Hits a mighty dry year, when de crab grass fail,
Oh, row, row, row, who laid dat rail?
Hit am mighty dark night when de nigger turn pale,
De big foot nigger what laid dat rail!
Oh, row, row, row, who laid dat rail?
Rinktum, ranktum, laid dat rail.
Show me de nigger what laid dat rail,
Oh, row, row, row, who laid dat rail?

"'When de niggers fuss, de white folks fail,
Oh, row, row, row, who laid dat rail?
We're gittin' dere now, don't tell no tale,
Show me de nigger what laid dat rail.
I'll stick he head in a big tin pail.
Oh, turn me loose, let me tech dat rail,
Oh, row, row, row, who laid dat rail?

"First us have white preachers and den, after freedom, de niggers starts to git up in meetin' and talk to sinners, and dey call dem 'Exhorters.' De white folks larnt de exhorters to read de Bible and some songs, and de niggers all larn de songs, too. De exhorter git up and read de scripture and it 'bout King Neb'kudneezer, when he have a golden image with silver horns, and all de kings and rulers come and bow down 'fore dat image, 'cepting three. Dem was Shadrach, Meshach, and Abednego. Dey would not bow down, so de old king throw dem in de furnace and dey not burn up, and dey say, 'De Gawd us worship am able to deliver us from de fiery furnace.'

Wayman Williams and Henry Freeman

"Den de exhorter say: 'Now, you no count niggers, what you mean stealin' de white folks chickens and watermillions? Dey ain't safe no longer dan de white man back am turned. Do you think Gawd would save you? No, sir! You be turned into de pillar of salt iffen you don't stop you unrighteous ways, and den where you be? You won't see no dancin' or hear no chickens hollerin'. Come on into de pearly gates and live right. Leave your stealin' and cussin' and dancin' to de debbil, and come to de mourners' bench.

"'Let de sun of salvation shine square on you face,
Fight de battles of de Lawd, fight soon and fight late,
And you'll allus find de latch to de golden gate.
No use for to wait till tomorrow,
De sun mustn't sot on you sorrow,
Sin's sharp as a bamboo briar,
Ask de Lawd for to fotch you up higher.'

"Dem songs was de gateway to enter, de pearly gateway. All de niggers git on de mourners' bench and git saved."

WILLIE WILLIAMS

Willie Williams, 78, was born a slave to Mr. William Maddox, who owned about 90 slaves, including Willie's parents, five brothers and a sister. The plantation was in Vermillion Parish, La., near Sparta. In 1867 Mr. Maddox took Willie, who was still working for him, to Texas. Willie now lives in Fort Worth.

"Dis nigger am 78 years old, and I's born in slavery, down in old Louisiana. Marster William owned me, and he am de father of Marster Ed Maddox what now runs de Maddox Milk and Ice Company here in Fort Worth. I knowed him when him and dis nigger am tiny chiles. I goes and visits with him often and we talks 'bout old times and sich. We laughs 'bout some things and de tears come in de eyes 'bout some things. Him allus give dis nigger de quarter or de half dollar for old times sake.

"Marster William owns sich a big plantation dat it was miles and miles 'round and had 'bout 90 grown nigger slaves. I 'members it well and sho' am glad for to tell yous 'bout it and how dey does. De marster have a two-story house for his family and de place look like a town with all de buildings. Dere was de nigger quarters with 30 cabins and de nursery for de young niggers, de sheds and de smokehouse for de meat. Den dey have de gin and de mill for to grin' de grist, de spinning house and de shoe shop.

"Marster have a nigger what make de shoes out of hides tanned dere off de cattle what am killed for meat. Him makes good shoes, they las' a long time, but they sure is tough on de feets.

"Marster William raises de corn and rice and wheat and barley and vegetables and honey, and lots of cotton. Dey works animals, de mules and de oxen, but I seed de niggers hitched to de plow sometimes. But de marster allus took good care of his niggers and him feeds plenty good victuals. Every Sunday dey measures out de rations, 'cept de vegetables. But if what dey give am not 'nough, we'uns calls for more. De marster wants for we'uns to have plenty.

"All us am given de pass for to go to de church or to de party and dere's a place near de quarters for de dance and sich. Some fool niggers sneaks off without de pass sometimes and gits catched by de patter rollers and gits couple passes from de whup.

"One time de niggers puts one on dem patter rollers. Dere am de dance and some niggers has no pass and de patter rollers am a-comin'. De niggers 'cide to best 'em and one gits de pan of hot ashes and when dem patter rollers comes to de door de ashes am thrown in de face. De niggers all rush out and knocks de rollers down, and de niggers am gone. Dats once de niggers 'prise de rollers.

"On dat plantation dere am sort of hospital fix for to care for de sick. Dey uses herbs and sich and sometimes calls de doctor. De small chillens is kep' dere and de marster sho' am 'ticular 'bout dem. Lots of times he look dem over and say, 'Dat one be worth a t'ousand dollars,' or 'Dat one be a whopper.' You see, 'twas jus' like raisin' young mules.

Willie Williams

"On dat plantation, dere am no weddin' 'lowed for to git married. Dey jus' gits married, but some not 'lowed to git married, 'cause de marster anxious to raise good, big niggers, de kind what am able to do lots of work and sell for a heap of money. Him have 'bout ten wenches him not 'low to git married and dey am big, strong women and de doctor 'xamine dem for de health. Den de marster picks out de big nigger and de doctor 'xamine him, too. Dat nigger do no work but watch dem womens and he am de husban' for dem all. De marster sho' was a-raisin' some fine niggers dat way.

"As for de whippin', dey gives dat punishment. Dey straps de nigger over de barrel but de marster don't 'low for to draw de blood.

"Durin' de War, dere am de shortage of food and one time we is 'bliged eat all de chickens, and 'twarnt hard to do. We hunts de wild hawg and wild turkey and de deer and sich.

"When freedom come, dey tell all us niggers we's free and we can stay or leave and work for wages if we stay. Three year after freedom de marster sells de plantation and comes to Fort Worth and I and five other niggers still with him. I works for him 'til he dies, 'bout 50 year ago."

LULU WILSON

Lulu Wilson, blind, bedridden Negro, does not know her age, but believes that she is ninety-seven. She was born near the Mammoth Cave, in Kentucky. Lulu owns a little home at 1108 Good Street, Dallas, Texas.

"Course I's born in slavery, ageable as I am. I'm a old time, slavery woman and the way I been through the hackles, I got plenty to say 'bout slavery. Lulu Wilson says she knows they ain't no good in it and they better not bring it back.

"My paw warn't no slave. He was a free man, 'cause his mammy was a full blood Creek Indian. But my maw was born in slavery, down on Wash Hodges' paw's place, and he give her to Wash when he married. That was the only woman slave what he had and one man slave, a young buck. My maw say she took with my paw and I's born, but a long time passed and didn't no more young'uns come, so they say my paw am too old and wore out for breedin' and wants her to take with this here young buck. So the Hodges sot the nigger hounds on my paw and run him away from the place and maw allus say he went to the free state. So she took with my step-paw and they must of pleased the white folks what wanted niggers to breed like livestock, 'cause she birthed nineteen chillen.

"When I's li'l I used to play in that big cave they calls Mammoth and I's so used to that cave it didn't seem like nothin' to me. But I was real li'l then, for soon as they could they put me to spinnin' cloth. I 'members plain, when I was li'l there was talk of war in them parts, and they put me to spinnin' and I heared 'em say it was for sojers. They marched round in a li'l, small drove and practices shootin'.

"Now, when I was li'l they was the hardes' times. They'd nearly beat us to death. They taken me from my mammy, out the li'l house built onto they house and I had to sleep in a bed by Missus Hodges. I cried for my maw but I had to work and wash and iron and clean and milk cows when I was most too li'l to do it.

"The Hodges had three chilluns and the olderes' one they was mean to, 'cause she so thickheaded. She couldn't larn nothin' out a book but was kinder and more friendly like than the rest of the lot. Wash Hodges was jes' mean, pore trash and he was a bad actor and a bad manager. He never could make any money and he starved it out'n the niggers. For years all I could git was one li'l slice of sowbelly and a puny, li'l piece of bread and a 'tater. I never had 'nough to stave the hongriness out'n my belly.

"My maw was cookin' in the house and she was a clink, that am the bes' of its kind. She could cuss and she warn't 'fraid. Wash Hodges tried to whop her with a cowhide and she'd knock him down and bloody him up. Then he'd go down to some his neighbor kin and try to git them to come help him whop her. But they'd say, 'I don't want to go up there and let Chloe Ann beat me up.' I heared Wash tell his wife they said that.

"When maw was in a tantrum, my step-paw wouldn't partialise with her. But she was a 'ligious woman and 'lieved time was comin' when niggers wouldn't be slaves. She told me to pray for it. She seed a old man what the nigger dogs chased and et the legs near off him. She said she was chased by them bloody hounds and she jus' picked up a club and laid they skull open. She say they hired her out and sold her twice but allus brung her back to Wash Hodges.

"Now, Missus Hodges studied 'bout meanness more'n Wash done. She was mean to anybody she could lay her hands to, but special mean to me. She beat me and used to tie my hands and make me lay flat on the floor and she put snuff in my eyes. I ain't lyin' 'fore Gawd when I say I knows that's why I went blind. I did see white folks sometimes what spoke right friendly and kindly to me.

"I gits to thinkin' now how Wash Hodges sold off maw's chillun. He'd sell 'em and have the folks come for 'em when my maw was in the fields. When she'd come back, she'd raise a ruckus. Then many the time I seed her plop right down to a settin' and cry 'bout it. But she 'lowed they warn't nothin' could be done, 'cause it's the slavery law. She said, 'O, Lawd, let me see the end of it 'fore I die, and I'll quit my cussin' and fightin' and rarin'.' My maw say she's part Indian and that 'countable for her ways.

"One day they truckled us all down in a covered wagon and started out with the fam'ly and my maw and step-paw and five of us chillun. I know I's past twelve year old. We come a long way and passed through a free State. Some places we druv for miles in the woods 'stead of the big road, and when we come to folks they hid us down in the bed of the wagon. We passed through a li'l place and my maw say to look, and I seed a man gwine up some steps, totin' a bucket of water. She say, 'Lulu, that man's your paw.' I ain't never think she's as consid'ble of my step-paw as of my paw, and she give me to think as much. My step-paw never did like me, but he was a fool for his own young'uns, 'cause at the end of the wars when they sot the niggers free, he tramped over half the country, gatherin' up them young'uns they done sold 'way.

"We went to a place called Wadefield, in Texas, and settled for some short passin' of time. They was a Baptist church next our house and they let me go twict. I was fancified with the singin' and preachin'. Then we goes on to Chatfield Point and Wash Hodges built a log house and covered it with weather boarding and built my maw and paw quarters to live in. They turned in to raisin' corn and 'taters and hawgs. I had to work like a dog. I hoed and milked ten cows a day.

"Missus told me I had ought to marry. She said if I'd marry she'd togger me up in a white dress and give me a weddin' supper. She made the dress and Wash Hodges married me out'n the Bible to a nigger 'longin' to a nephew of his'n. I was 'bout thirteen or fourteen. I know it warn't long after that when Missus Hodges got a doctor to me. The doctor told me less'n I had a baby, old as I was and married, I'd start in on spasms. So it warn't long till I had a baby.

"In 'twixt that time, Wash Hodges starts layin' out in the woods and swamps all the time. I heared he was hidin' out from the war and was sposed to go, 'cause he done been a volunteer in the first war and they didn't have no luck in Kentucky.

"One night when we was all asleep, some folks whooped and woke us up. Two sojers come in and they left more outside. They found Wash Hodges and said it was midnight and to git 'em something to eat. They et and some more come in and et. They tied Wash's hands and made me hold a lamp in the door for them to see by. They had some more men in the wagon, with they hands tied. They druv away and in a minute I heared the reports of the guns three or four times. Nex' day I heared they was sojers and done shot some conscripts in the bottoms back of our place.

"Wash Hodges was gone away four years and Missus Hodges was meaner'n the devil all the time. Seems like she jus' hated us worser than ever. She said blobber-mouth niggers done cause a war.

"Well, now, things jus' kind of drifts along for a spell and then Wash Hodges come back and he said, 'Well, now, we done whop the hell out them blue bellies and that'll larn 'em a lesson to leave us alone.'

Lulu Wilson

"Then my step-paw seed some Fed'ral sojers. I seed them, too. They drifted by in droves of fifty and a hundred. My step-paw 'lowed as how the Feds done told him they ain't no more slavery, and he tried to pint it out to

Wash Hodges. Wash says that's a new ruling, and it am that growed-up niggers is free, but chillun has to stay with they masters till they's of age.

"My maw was in her cabin with a week old baby and one night twelve Klu Kluxses done come to the place. They come in by ones and she whopped 'em one at a time.

"I don't never recall just like, the passin' of time. I know I had my little boy young'un and he growed up, but right after he was born I left the Hodges and felt like it's a fine, good riddance. My boy died, but he left me a grandson. He growed up and went to 'nother war, and they done somethin' to him and he ain't got but one lung. He ain't peart no more. He's got four chillun and he makes fifty dollars a month. I'm crazy 'bout that boy and he comes to see me, but he can't help me none in a money way. So I'm right grateful to the president for gittin' my li'l pension. I done study it out in my mind for three years and tell him, Lulu says if he will see they ain't no more slavery, and if they'll pay folks liveable wages, they'll be less stealin' and slummerin' and goin's on. I worked so hard. For more'n fifty years I waited as a nurse on sick folks. I been through the hackles if any mortal soul has, but it seems like the president thinks right kindly of me, and I want him to know Lulu Wilson thinks right kindly of him."

WASH WILSON

Wash Wilson, 94, was born a slave of Tom Wilson, in Louisiana, near the Ouachita Road. Wash and his family were purchased by Bill Anderson, who brought them to Robertson Co., Texas. Wash lives in Eddy, Texas.

"I was 'bout eighteen years old when de Civil war come. Us calls it de Freedom War. I was born in Louisiana, clost to de Ouachita Road, and Marse Tom Wilson owned mammy and us chillen. But Marse Bill Anderson he come from Texas to buy us from Marse Tom. Marse Tom, he 'lowed de gov'ment gwine let dem damn Yankees give de South a whuppin' and dere wasn't gwine be no slaves nowhere. But Marse Bill say we's a likely bunch of chillen and mammy am a grand cook, so guess he take de resk.

"Marse Tom starts to Texas where he had a passel of land. Us was sold on de block to him, 'cause Marse Tom say he gwine git all he done put in us out us, iffen he can 'fore de Yanks take dis country.

"Mammy was named Julia Wilson. Sis Sally was oldest of us chillen, den brudder Harry and me. Marse Bill he had 27,000 acres of land in Robertson County what he git for fightin' Indians and sech. He lived in seven mile of Calvert, Texas, and dat where he brunged us and de supplies and sech. Us traveled in ox carts and hoss back, and de mos' us niggers walked.

"Us was sot free on de road to Texas. Us camp one night and some folks come talk with Marse Bill. De next mornin' he told us, 'Boys, you's free as I is.' Us was only 'bout sixteen mile from where us gwine and Marse Bill say, 'All what want to stay with me can.' Us didn't know nobody and didn't have nothin' and us liked Marse Bill, so all us stayed with him. When we got to his place us did round and 'bout, clearin' new ground and buildin' cabins and houses. Dere was three log houses but us had to build more.

"My pappy name was Bill Wilson. All my folks am dead now, but on de plantation in Louisiana we had a good time. Mammy could cook and spin and weave. Dey raised cotton and sugar cane and corn.

"Dere wasn't many Indians when us come, in our part de country. All I ever saw jes' steal and beg. Dere was plenty wild turkeys and wild hawgs and deer and prairie chickens.

"On Marse Bill's place every quarters had its barn and mule, but Marse and he wife, Miss Deborah, lived in de quality quarters. Round dem was de blacksmith shop and smokehouse and spinnin' house and Marse Bill have a li'l house jus' for he office. De cookhouse was a two-room house side de big house with a covered passage to de dinin' room. De milk house was de back part de cook house.

"In de smokehouse was hams and sides of hawg meat and barrels of syrup and sugar and lard, and bushels of onions, and de 'tater room was allus full. Dey dug a big place and put poles and pieces of cane and lumber cross, like a top, and put dirt and leaves and banked de dirt round de 'tater room. Dey'd leave a place to crawl in, but dey kep' it tight and dem 'taters dey kep' most all winter.

"Dey was hayricks and chicken roosties and big lye hoppers where us put all de fireplace ashes. Come de rain and de water run through dat hopper into de trough under it, and dat make lye water. De women put old meat skins and bones and fat in de big, iron pot in de yard and put in some lye water and bile soap. Den dey cut it when it git cold and put it on de smokehouse shelves to dry. Dat sho' fine soap.

"Mammy worked in de kitchen mostly and spin by candlelight. Dey used a bottle lamp. Dat a rag or piece of big string, stuck in de snuff bottle full of tallow or grease. Later on in de years, dey used coal oil in de bottles. Sometimes dey wrap a rag round and round and put it in a pan of grease, and light dat for de lamp. Dey used pine torches, too.

"De black folks' quarters was log cabins, with stick and dirt chimneys. Dey had dere own garden round each cabin and some chickens, but dere wasn't no cows like in Louisiana. Dere was lots of possums in de bottoms and us go coon and possum huntin'. I likes cornbread and greens, cook with de hawg jowls or strip bacon. Dat's what I's raised on. Us had lots of lye hominy dem days. Marse Bill, he gwine feed everybody good on his place. Den us had ash cake, make of corn meal. Us didn't buy much till long time after de War.

"Us had poles stuck in de corner and tied de third pole cross, to make de bed. Dey called 'Georgia Hosses'. Us filled ticks with corn shucks or crab grass and moss. Dey wasn't no cotton beds for de niggers, 'cause dey wasn't no gins for de long time and de cotton pick from de seed by hand and dat slow work. De white folks had cotton beds and feather beds and wool beds.

"Marse Bill allus had de doctor for us iffen de old woman couldn't git us well. All de seven families Marse Bill done buy in Louisiana stayed round him and he family till dey all dead, white and cullud. I's de onlies' one left.

"Us piled 'bout a hundred or two or maybe three hundred bushels corn outside de shed. Us have corn shuckin' at night and have de big time. De fellow what owned de corn, he give a big supper and have all de whiskey us want. Nobody got drunk, 'cause most everybody carry dey liquor purty well. After shuckin' us have ring plays. For music dey scratch on de skillet lids or beat bones or pick de banjo. Dere be thirty to fifty folks, all cullud, and sometimes dey stay all night, and build de big fire and dance outdoors or in de barn.

"Dere wasn't no music instruments. Us take pieces a sheep's rib or cow's jaw or a piece iron, with a old kettle, or a hollow gourd and some horsehairs to make de drum. Sometimes dey'd git a piece of tree trunk and hollow it out and stretch a goat's or sheep's skin over it for de drum. Dey'd be one to four foot high and a foot up to six foot 'cross. In gen'ral two niggers play with de fingers or sticks on dis drum. Never seed so many in Texas, but dey made some. Dey'd take de buffalo horn and scrape it out to make de flute. Dat sho' be heared a long ways off. Den dey'd take a mule's jawbone and rattle de stick 'cross its teeth. Dey'd take a barrel and stretch a ox's hide 'cross one end and a man sot 'stride de barrel and beat on dat hide with he hands, and he feet, and iffen he git to feelin' de music in he bones, he'd beat on dat barrel with he head. 'Nother man beat one wooden side with sticks. Us 'longed to de church, all right, but dancin' ain't sinful iffen de foots ain't crossed. Us danced at de arbor meetin's but us sho' didn't have us foots crossed!

"When de niggers go round singin' 'Steal Away to Jesus,' dat mean dere gwine be a 'ligious meetin' dat night. Dat de sig'fication of a meetin'. De masters 'fore and after freedom didn't like dem 'ligious meetin's, so us natcherly slips off at night, down in de bottoms or somewheres. Sometimes us sing and pray all night.

"I voted till I's 'bout forty five year old, den I jes' kinder got out de habit.

"I got married in a suit of doeskin jeans, ain't none like dem nowadays. I married Cornelia Horde and she wore a purty blue gingham de white folks buyed and made for her. Us had six chillen, Calvin and Early and Mary and Fred and Frank.

"Iffen you knows someone workin' a conjure trick 'gainst you, jes' take some powdered brick and scrub the steps real good. Dat'll kill any conjure spell, sho'. De bes' watchdog you can get for de hoodoo is a frizzly chicken. Iffen you got one dem on de place, you can rest in peace, 'cause it scratches up every trick lay down 'gainst its owner. Iffen you see dat frizzly chicken scratchin' round de place, it a sho' sign you been conjured. A frizzly chicken come out he shell backwards, and day why he de devil's own.

"De old folks allus told me to make a cross inside my

shoe every mornin' 'fore leavin' de house, den ain't no conjurer gwine git he conjure 'gainst you foots. Iffen you wear you under clothes wrong side out, you can't be conjured. 'nother way am to put saltpetre in de soles you shoes. Iffen you wears a li'l piece de 'peace plant' in you pocket or you shoe, dat powerful strong 'gainst conjure. A piece of de Betsy bug's heart with some silver money am good. But iffen you can't git none dose, jes' take a piece newspaper and cut it de size of you shoe sole and sprinkle nine grains red pepper on it. Dere ain't no hoodoo gwine ever harm you den, 'cause he'd have to stop and count every letter on dat newspaper and by dat time, you gwine be 'way from dere.

Wash Wilson

"Iffen you want to find de conjure tricks what done been sot for you, jes' kill you a fat chicken and sprinkle some its blood in da conjure doctor's left palm. Den take you forefinger and hit dat blood till it spatter, and it gwine spatter in da direction where dat trick am hid. Den when you find de trick, sprinkle a li'l quicksilver over a piece of paper and put da paper on de fire, and dat trick gwine be laid forever.

"Old folks done told me how to make a conjurer leave town. Make up a hick'ry fire and let it burn down to coals. Den you take up two live coals. One dese gwine be you, and de other gwine be de luck. Take up one dead coal, and dat you enemy. Den you jes' keep 'wake till de rooster crow or midnight. Dat am de end of de day. Now you chunk de live coal what am you to de south, de warm country; den throw de other live coal to de east; den chunk de dead coal, you enemy, to de north, de cold country. Nothin' of de conjurer can't git over fire, and 'fore de week out, dat conjurer be leavin'.

"A old Indian who used to hang round Marse Bill's place say to git de best of a conjurer, git some clay from da mouth a crawfish hole, and some dirt from a red ant's hole. Mix dem and wet dem with whiskey or camphor. Git some angleworms and boil dem and add de worm water to de clay and dirt. Iffen you rubs de conjured pusson with dis, he trouble done go 'way."

WILLIS WINN

Willis Winn claims to be 116 years old. He was born in Louisiana, a slave of Bob Winn, who Willis says taught him from his youth that his birthday was March 10, 1822. When he was freed Willis and his father moved to Hope, Arkansas, where they lived sixteen years. Willis then moved to Texarkana and from there to Marshall, where he has lived fourteen years. Willis lives alone in a one-room log house in the rear of the Howard Vestal home on the Powder Mill Road, north of Marshall, and is supported by an $11.00 per month old age pension.

"The onliest statement I can make 'bout my age is my old master, Bob Winn, allus told me if anyone ask me how old I is to say I's borned on March the tenth, in 1822. I's knowed my birthday since I's a shirt-tail boy, but can't figure in my head.

"My pappy was Daniel Winn and he come from Alabama, and I 'member him allus sayin' he'd like to go back there and get some chestnuts. Mammy was named Patsy and they was nine of us chillen. The five boys was me and Willie and Hosea and two Georges, and the gals was Car'lina and Dora and Anna and Ada, and all us lived to be growed and have chillen.

"Massa Bob's house faced the quarters where he could hear us holler when he blowed the big horn for us to git up. All the houses was made of logs and we slept on shuck and grass mattresses what was allus full of chinches. I still sleep on a grass mattress, 'cause I can't rest on cotton and feather beds.

"We et yellow bread and greens and black-eyed peas and potlicker and sopped 'lasses. Us and the white folks all cooked in fireplaces. A big iron pot hung out in the yard for to bile greens and hog jowl and sich like. We didn't know nothing 'bout bakin' powder and made our soda from burnt cobs. That's jes' as good soda as this Arm and Hammer you get in the store. We et flour bread Sundays, but you daren't git cotch with flour dough 'cept on that day. Mammy stole lots of it, though. She rolled it up and put it round her head and covered it with her head-rag. Wild game was all over the country, buffalo and bears and panthers and deer and possum and coon. The squirrels 'most run over you in the woods. We et at a long, wooden trough and it was allus clean and full of plenty grub. We used buffalo and fish bones for spoons, and some et with they hands. The grub I liked best was whatever I could git.

Us slaves didn't wear nothing but white lowell cloth. They give us pants for Sunday what had a black stripe down the leg. The chillen wore wool clothes in winter, but the big folks wore the same outfit the year round. They didn't care if you froze.

"I can show you right where I was when the stars fell. Some say they covered the ground like snow, but nary one ever hit the ground. They fell in 'bout twelve feet of the ground. The chillen jumped up and tried to cotch them. I don't 'member how long they fell, but they was shootin' through the air like sky-rockets fer quite a spell.

"Missy Callie had one gal and two boys and Massa Bob had three overseers. He didn't have nigger drivers, but had his pets. We called them pimps, 'cause they was allus tattlin' when we done anything. His place was jes' as far as you could let your eyes see, 'bout 1,800 or 1,900 acres, and he owned more'n 500 niggers.

"I still got the bugle he woke us with at four in the mornin'. When the bugle blowed you'd better go to hollerin', so the overseer could hear you. If he had to call you, it was too bad. The first thing in the mornin' we'd go to the lot and feed, then to the woodpile till breakfast. They put our grub in the trough and give us so long to eat. Massa hollered if we was slow eatin'. 'Swallow that grub now and chaw it tonight. Better be in that field by daybreak.' We worked from see to can't.

"I's seed many a nigger whipped on a 'buck and gag' bench. They buckled 'em down hard and fast on a long bench, gagged they mouth with cotton and when massa got through layin' on that cowhide, the blood was runnin' off on the ground. Next mornin' after he whip you, he'd come to the quarters when you git up and say, 'Boy, how is you feelin'? No matter how sore you is, you'd better jump and kick you heels and show how lively you is.' Massa hated me to he dying day, 'cause I told missy 'bout him whippin' a gal scandously in the field, 'cause she want to go to the house to her sick baby. Missy Callie didn't whip us, but she'd twist our nose and ears nearly off. Them fingers felt like a pair of pinchers. She stropped on her guns and rode a big bay horse to the field.

"Massa had a gin and I hauled cotton to Port Caddo, on Caddo Lake. I druv eight mules and hauled eight bales of cotton. Massa followed me with two mules and two bales of cotton. I usually had a good start of him. The patterrollers has cotched me and unhitched my mules and druv 'em off, leavin' me in the middle of the road. They'd start back home, but when they overtook massa they stopped, 'cause he druv the lead mules. He fetched 'em back and say, 'Willis, what happen?' He sho' cussed them patterrollers and said he'll git even yet.

"They was sellin' slaves all the time, puttin' 'em on the block and sellin' 'em, 'cordin' to how much work they could do in a day and how strong they was. I's seed lots of 'em in chains like cows and mules. If a owner have more'n he needed, he hit the road with 'em and sold 'em off to 'joinin' farms. None of 'em ever run off. They couldn't git away. I's seed too many try it. If the patterrollers didn't cotch you, some white folks would put you up and call your massa. They had a 'greement to be on the watch fer runaway niggers. When the massa git you back home and git through with you, you'd sho' stay home.

"In slavery time the niggers wasn't 'lowed to look at a book. I larned to read and write after surrender in the jail at Hot Springs, in Arkansas.

"They give us cake at Christmas and eggnog and 'silly-bug'. Eggnog is made from whites of eggs and 'silly-bug' from yallers. You have to churn the whiskey and yallers to make 'silly-bug'.

"Corn shuckin's was the things them days. I liked to see 'em come. They cooked up guineas and ducks and chickens and sometimes roast a pig. Massa kept twenty, thirty barrels whiskey round over the place all the time, with tin cups hangin' on the barrels. You could drink when you want to, but sho' better not git drunk. Massa have to watch he corners when cornshuckin' am over, or us niggers grab him and walk him round in the air on their hands.

"When some of the white folks died every nigger on the place had to go to the grave and walk round and drap in some dirt on him. They buried the niggers anyway. Dig a ditch and cover 'em up. I can show you right now down in Louisiana where I was raised, forty acres with nothin' but niggers buried on 'em.

"I 'member lots 'bout the war but can't tell you all, 'cause every war have its secrets. That war had four salutes, and you'd better give the right one when you meet the captain. I's heared the niggers sing, 'Gonna hang Jeff Davis to a sour apple tree.' My pappy fought in the last battle, at Mansfield, and so did Massa Bob.

"When the 'Federates come in sight of Mansfield they was carryin' a red flag, and kept it raised till surrender. When the Yanks come in sight they raised a white flag and wanted the 'Federates to surrender, but they wouldn't answer. It wasn't long till the whole world round there smelt like powder. Guns nowadays jus' goes 'pop-pop', but them guns sounded like thunder.

"After surrender, massa freed the men and missy freed the women, but he didn't let us loose when he ought. They wasn't no places 'vided with niggers as I heared 'bout. Niggers in Louisiana say Queen Elizabeth sent a boatload of gold to America to give the free men, but we never seed any of it. Massa give us each a barrel meal, a barrel flour, a side of meat and ten gallons 'lasses and tell us we can work for who we pleases. Daddy bought two cows and a horse and eight hawgs and a goat from massa on credit and we moved and made three crops.

"The Yanks stayed round Louisiana a long time after surrender. They come to white folks houses what hadn't freed they slaves and busted they meal and flour barrels and burn they meat and say, 'If we have to face you 'gain, we'll sweep you from the cradle up.'

"I's been cotched by them Ku Kluxers. They didn't hurt me, but have lots of fun makin' me cut capers. They pulls my clothes off once and make me run 'bout four hunerd yards and stand on my head in the middle the road.

"They is plenty niggers in Louisiana that is still slaves. A spell back I made a trip to where I was raised, to see my old missy 'fore she died, and there was niggers in twelve or fourteen miles of that place that they didn't know they is free. They is plenty niggers round here what is same as slaves, and has worked for white folks twenty and twenty-five years and ain't drawed a five cent piece, jus' old clothes and somethin' to eat. That's the way we was in slavery.

"Bout four years after surrender pappy say he heared folks say gold was covering the ground at Hope, Arkansas, so we pulled up and moved there. We found lots of money where they'd been a big camp, but no gold. We lived there sixteen years, then I came to Texarkana and worked twelve years for G.W. George Fawcett's sawmill. I never married till I was old, in Little Washington, Arkansas, and lived with my wife thirty-six years 'fore she died. We raised eighteen chillen to be growed and nary one of 'em was ever arrested.

Willis Winn

"I was allus wild and played for dances, but my wife was 'ligious and after I married I quieted down. When I jined the church, I burned my fiddle up. I allus made a livin' from public road work since I left Texarkana, till I got no count for work. The only time I voted was in Hope, and I voted the 'publican ticket and all my folks got mad.

"If it wasn't for the good white folks, I'd starved to death. 'Fore I come here to the Vestals, I was livin' in a shack on the T. & P. tracks and I couldn't pay no rent. I was sick and the woman made me git out. Master Vestal found me down by the tracks, eatin' red clay. I'd lived for three days on six tomatoes. I et two a day. Master Vestal went home and his wife cooked a big pot of stew, with meat and potatoes, and fetched it to me. Then they built a house down behind their back yard and I's lived with 'em ever since.

"I allus say the cullud race started off wrong when they was freed and is still wrong today. They had a shot to be well off, but they can't keep money. You give one a bank of money and he'll be busted tomorrow. I tells young niggers every day they ought to come down where they'll have some sense. I serves the Lord at home and don't meddle with 'em."

RUBE WITT

Rube Witt, 87, was a slave of Jess Witt of Harrison County, Texas. He enlisted in the Confederate Army at Alexandria, La., and was sent to Mansfield, but his regiment arrived after the victory of the North. He worked for his master for a year after the war, then moved to Marshall and worked for Edmund Key, Sr., pioneer banker and civic leader. Rube cooked for eighteen years at the old Capitol Hotel in Marshall, and took up preaching as a side line. He and his wife live at 707 E. Crockett St., in Marshall. They receive a $15.00 pension.

"I was born on the Jess Witt place, right here in Harrison County, on the tenth day of August, in 1850, and allus lived in and round Marshall. My father and mother, Daniel and Jane, was bred and born in Texas, and belonged to the Witts. I had five brothers, named Charlie and Joe and George and Bill and Jim, and six sisters, named Mary and Susan and Betsy and Anna and Effie and Lucinda. They all lived to be growed but I'm the onliest chile still livin'.

"Master Witt had a big place, I don't recall how many acres. He didn't have so many slaves. Slavery was a tight fight. We lived in li'l cabins and slept on rough plank beds and et bacon and peas and pa'ched corn. We didn't hardly know what flour bread was. Master give us one outfit of clothes to a time and sometimes shoes. We worked all day in the fields, come in and fed the stock and did the chores and et what li'l grub it took to do us and went to bed. You'd better not go nowhere without a pass, 'cause them patterrollers was rolling round every bush.

"My missus was named Kate and had two chillen. The Witts had a good set of niggers and didn't have to whip much. Sometimes he give us a light brushin' for piddlin' round at work. I seed plenty niggers whipped on ole man Ruff Perry and Pratt Hughes places, though. They was death on 'em. Lawyer Marshall used to whip his niggers goin' and comin' every day that come round.

"I 'members white folks sayin' war was startin' 'bout keepin' slaves and then I seed 'em mendin' the harness and wagons to go and fight. I was the houseboy for the Witts durin' the war and 'bout time it was over I enlisted at Alexandria as a soldier and they sent me to Mansfield. The Yanks had done won the victory when our reg'ment got there. They turned us loose to git home the best we could. I come back to the Witts and master calls up all the slaves and says we was free, but if we stayed and worked for him we'd have plenty to eat and wear, and if we left, it'd be root, hawg or die. Most of 'em left but I stayed a year. You'd ought to seed 'em pullin' off them croaker-sack clothes when master says we's free.

"I come to Marshall with my mother and the whole state was under United States law. The 8th Regiment of Illinois was at Marshall for two years after the war, and no man, black, white or red or what is you, darsn't git cotched after dark without a pass. When they'd stop you, if you couldn't give the U.S. sign, 'Grant's Friend,' they'd shoot the devil out of you. You didn't pass 'less you knowed the sign.

"The Confederates had a big gun powder mill on Mill's Creek, two and a half miles north of Marshall and it stayed operatin' two or three years. But Gen. Atichon and Capt. Bishop and Lt. Rives and a bunch of Yanks tried to capture it and the Confederates blowed it up.

"When I was 'bout sixteen my mother hires me out to a Mr. Acorns, who was refugeed from Georgia to Marshall. Ole man Acorns was a mile of hell anywhere you met him and he nearly beat me to death and I run away. His son and him and 'nother man starts after me and I has to light a shuck. We sho' had some race down that hill over where the new water tower is in Sunny South, but they didn't cotch me. The white folks round here didn't 'lieve us niggers was free then.

Rube Witt

"Then I goes to work for Mr. Edmond Key, Sr., and stays with him till I'm growed. I used to help chase rabbits where the court house is now. I recalls the Buzzard Roost Hotel and some stores was on that square then.

"I cooks for the old Capitol Hotel eighteen years, then I quit and tries railroadin', but it didn't take long to decide to go back to the cook apron. I allus made a livin' from cookin' and preachin', and I've preached forty-five years. The only times I voted was for high sheriff once and for President Garfield and President Grant.

"I marries in 1915 and my wife is still with me. I'm too stove up with rhumatis' now to work and her and me gits $15.00 a month from the government."

United States. Work Projects Administration

RUBEN WOODS

Ruben Woods, hale and strong despite his 84 years, was born a slave of the John Woods family in Taladiga County, Alabama. He served as houseboy in their home until he was 21, then came to Tyler, Texas, with one of his master's children. He now lives in El Paso, Texas.

"I'se de oldest of seven chillen. My father was John Woods, mother Laura Woods. She was a cook for de marster's family on de plantation. We lived in a log house, logs was hewed in de woods. De marster's house was plastered inside. He had 1,000 acres plantation and 96 slaves. He took good care of 'em. Onct a week dey would come and dey allowanced 'em out pervisions. Not fine stuff; no, dey didn' gib 'em nothin' like dat ham and such. Dey would gib you enough flour for biscuit for Sunday mornin' and dey gib potatoes. I tell you how dey done dat; ev'ry family, he had a basket and when dey blow de ho'n in de evenin' ev'ry chile dat was big enough come and he know his basket and take it home.

"De quarters was all in rows. You had to have a pass frum de massa to go from one place to anudder or the pateroller would ketch you and whop you. Overseers whopped 'em, too.

"You worked frum time you could see 'till dark. You

couldn' git outta dat, no suh, time you coul' see de stuff in de fiel', you was out workin.'

"Ole man Woods was a powerful good man. He wouldn' raise cotton for sale, only jus' enough for de women to make clothes. He raised hogs and cattle. I 'member Ben Averit; he had a big plantation over on de island. Took boatloads of slaves and work 'em hard. We'd hear de boats go over, clop-clop.

"We'd take two yoke of oxen with co'n and wheat to de mill, stay all day, den bring it back to give ev'rybody. I go to mill lots of times and allus drive oxen. In hot weather, dey run off to de creek. What you talkin' erbout, when it gits hot and dey smell dat water, dey travel!

"I 'member stagecoach. Had erbout six or eight hosses to 'em. Driver'd blow bugle for stops jus' like trains. Dey didn' have much trains dem days.

"When de war comes, we had soldiers. I se'ed 'em drillin' and marchin'. I se'ed dem hep-hep-hep! Yes, ma'am, when de Yanks come we was a runnin' and a squattin' like partridges a hidin'. Dem guns was a firin' and shootin' dem cannon, spoilin' fiel's and killin' hawgs. Wasn't no fun. Drums a beatin'. It was excitable, yes, ma'am. We had to run and hide. We all run up to whut dey call a cave and down in dat cave we had eats. All come what could git in dere. De soldiers try to roun' 'em up, but not dem niggers. All run from one place to anudder.

"I learned to read and write after freedom. Dey not allow you no book larnin'. Obey your marster and missus, dat's all.

"I 'member jist as well as dat I'se sittin' here, when

freedom come. Marster had 'em all come near de gate and he say, 'You all is free as I am now.' He hollered and cried. It tickled me to see him cry. And den he say, 'But now iffen you want to, all kin stay and finish up de crop. I'll feed you.' Some, dey go to de neighbors. Dey didn' know whut to do. Dey hadn' been taught to do for demselves. But dey couldn' whop 'em no more. I stayed 'till I was 21.

Ruben Woods

"No, ma'am, I never coul' sing, but I 'member one song. It went dis way:

>'1821—Jesus work is jus' begun;
>1822—Jesus brought de sinner through;
>1823—Jesus sot de prisoner free;
>1824—Jesus preached 'mong de poor;
>1825—Jesus brought de dead to life;
>1826—Jesus had all things fixed;
>1827—Jesus rose and went to Heben;
>1828—Jesus made de plain way straight;
>1829—Jesus turned de blood to wine.'

"We played hide-a-hoop. And hide-a-switch. We do dis; you'se huntin' switch and gittin' hot, gittin' col', dey take after you, dey have a base to go to. Den if dey ketch dem dey whop 'em.

"We played 'Anthony Over,' wid thread balls. We throw dat ball over de house. If dey don' ketch it, dey's out. Dat's de way dey had de sport."

WILLIS WOODSON

Willis Woodson does not know his age, but looks very aged. He was born in Whiterock, but he does not know its location, except that it was somewhere east of the Mississippi River. Willis now lives in Tyler, Texas.

"I'm borned at a place called Whiterock, but don't rightly 'member no other name, but it was a long, long way from here, though. I was the prop'ty of Marse Richards, but he sold me and my maw and a lot of darkies to Marse Ike Isom. Maw said Marse Ike done pay $500 for me, cheap 'cause I's purty little and couldn't do much work.

"Marse Isom moved to Texas and everybody helped load de wagons, and we starts real early in a cold mornin'. De old womens and little chillens rode in de wagons, but de men walked. We traveled real slow, though, and it wasn't no worse'n plowin' all day. One Marse Isom's sons rid behind on a big, white hoss, and seed none of the darkies runned off. At night we fixes a supper and goes to bed and all de niggers is chained together and slept on straw beds. The white men tooked turns guardin' dem with guns.

"We gits to de new farm, long ways from where we lives befo', and starts clearin' land. When we gits settled,

Old Miss picks me to be nuss to her chillen. Maw didn't work in de field. She say she done been hurt when she got a whippin' when she ain't growed, and her back ain't good no more. Old Miss say, 'Eva, you come in de kitchen and make some chittlin's, and iffen you cooks good, you can work in my kitchen.' Maw, she make dem chitlin's and dey's damn good, so she gits to cook den.

"Marse and Old Miss lives in de big house, with boards outside, 'steadin' logs. It have big rooms, lots of dem, and a big fireplace all 'cross de side one room. Me and 'nother boy has to bring in logs to build de fire, him totin' one end and me totin' one end. I stays in de house, so I gits good clothes and shoes, too. Some dem niggers didn't have hardly no clothes, though,

"De mostest fun I ever got was when Marse Isom 'lows me to be footman. He gits me a uniform, most like a sojer's, 'ceptin' mine am red with black stripes down de pants. I 'member it jist like yesterday, de first time I puts it on. Marse give a cel'bration at he house and de doorman am sick, so I has to be it. He give me dat suit and say to hurry put it on. Den he make me come to de front door and let him in over and over, so as to git de hang of it. He told me to take his hat and cane and put dem up, and to say, 'Thank you,' and 'Dis way, please,' and not to say no more to nobody, and I didn't. After dat night I opens de door lots of times, but mostest I wears dat suit when I takes de white folks to church, while dey listens to preachin' and I holds de hosses.

Willis Woodson

"I never did see no niggers whipped, but I done see dat whip hangin' in de barn. It a big, long thing, lots bigger'n a horsewhip, and I know it must have been used, 'cause it all wore out at one end.

"All de fun we has am huntin' and fishin'. We can go any night if we gits a permit from Marse Isom. Sometimes at night, he lets all de big niggers git together 'hind de cabins and make a big bonfire. Den we sings all de songs we knows, till nine o'clock, den Marse rings de bell, to cut out all de noise.

"Jus' befo' dat war am over, some soldiers marches through de farm and kilt all de cows and stock and burns de barn, Marse beg dem not to burn he house, so dey didn't. Some dem niggers quits when dey freed, without no supper, but not dis nigger! I stays sev'ral years, den gits a job snakin' logs in a sawmill. Den I marries and has seven chillen and I stays with first one, den 'nother. I holps dem all I can. I been patchin' up some fishin' tackle today."

JAMES G. WOORLING

James G. Woorling, of Fort Worth, Texas, tells the story of Uncle Dave, one of the slaves that belonged to Mr. Woorling's father, who owned a large plantation near Point, in Rains County, Texas. The story relates how Uncle Dave provided for his family after they were freed, and is valuable as an example of how many ex-slaves managed to secure a foothold in a world for which slavery had not prepared them.

"During pre-war days my father owned a plantation near Point, in Rains County, as well as a large number of slaves, including one Uncle Dave. After the Negroes were emancipated, my father placed a large number of them on tracts of land within the plantation and furnished them with a mule team, a few sheep, some chickens, and the implements needed to cultivate the land. The Negroes were privileged to occupy the land for seven years and to keep whatever they made during that time. After the expiration of the seven years they were to pay in money or percentage of crops for the use of the land. This plan was followed by a number of plantation owners.

"Uncle Dave was an exceptional Negro. He was a natural mechanic, but could do carpenter work, blacksmithing, shoemaking and many other things equally well. He was a good manager, frugal and industrious, and it is doubtful if he paid out $50.00 in a year's time for food, clothing and other necessities during the seven years that he lived on the seventy-five acres on our plantation.

"He never bought a horsecollar, but made them himself, shaping them to prevent galling and packing them with corn husks. He made the hames from oak timber and made the metal accessories.

"The shoes for Dave's family he made from hides of animals slaughtered for the meat supply. About the only farm implements he bought were those that required high grade steel.

"Aunt Julia, his wife, did her part. She was adept at cooking and preserving, and knew how to cure meat. Salt and spices were purchased, but they raised barley and roasted it, to use in the place of tea or coffee. They raised sugar and ribbon cane and made their own sugar and molasses. Aunt Julia told father that eggs were traded for any articles of food that could not be obtained from the farm.

"Following the Civil War the production of cloth by power driven machines enabled manufacturers to sell cloth at a price that did not warrant continuance of the hand method. But that did not interest Dave and Julia. They had a spinning wheel and a loom made by Uncle Dave himself, and they made all the cloth needed by the family, dying it with the bark of blackoak, cherry or other trees.

"When the seven year period ended, my father thought that Uncle Dave would stay on the land. He had cleared it, built a house and barn and other structures, which all belonged to my father under the agreement. But

Uncle Dave was not interested in renting the land. He had saved enough money to buy a thousand acres between the towns of Point and Emory. He built a house and barn and moved his family.

"Uncle Dave came home one day from a trip to town with a load of cotton. He had a ten gallon keg, which he painted black. He cut a slit in the side of the keg and made a plug for the hole and told Julia the keg was to hold his surplus cash.

"Uncle Dave hid the keg and during the next twenty years refused to tell his wife, children or anyone else where it was. It is obvious that all the money he received for his crops, except a small sum, was surplus. Julia often asked Uncle Dave to tell her where the keg was, and told my father that Uncle Dave had not been well and she feared the possibility of his dying without disclosing the secret. Not long after, Uncle Dave was found dead one morning. Money was needed for funeral expenses, but the keg could not be found and Julia had to borrow the required amount.

"The family searched first in the more likely locations, then made a minute search of the whole place, but the keg was never found. On Uncle Dave's farm a fortune is cached. The keg must have long ago disintegrated, but the gold and silver money, the savings of twenty years, remain in their hiding place."

United States. Work Projects Administration

CAROLINE WRIGHT

Caroline Wright, about 90 years old, was born near Baton Rouge, Louisiana. Dr. Warren Wortham owned her parents and their 14 children. Caroline was 12 when they were freed. Her father, Robert Vaughn, moved to Texas, [HW: with master, p.2, para. 4 & 5] where he prospered and bought more than 300 acres of Tehuacana bottom land in McLennan County. Caroline and her husband now live at 59 Grant St., Waco, in a little house they bought after their family was grown.

"I was bo'ned in Louisiana on Jones Creek, by Baton Rouge, 'bout 90 years ago. I disremember the year. My pappy was Bob Vaughn and my mammy was Rose Ann. Dey was bo'ned by Baton Rouge. I had six sisters, Betsy Ann, Lydia, Nancy, Paga and Louisan; and three brothers, Horace, Robert and Tom. We was all owned by Dr. Warren Wortham and his wife, Annie. Mr. Bob, de doctor's brother, had us in charge, and he hired us out to Hays White, who owned a sugar plantation on de Mississippi River by Baton Rouge. Us all stayed at his place two year. Dere was sugar cane, co'n, peas and tomatoes raised on de farm. We lived in a log cabin made of pine logs and our beds was made outta pine timber with co'n shucks tacked on de bed, and our kivers was feather beds.

"In Clinton, in Louisiana, we was all put on de block and valued. I was six year old and I was valued at $1,500.

But our family wasn' sold to anyone. I was given to Miss Muriel, Dr. Wortham's daughter. Me and my sisters was made house slaves and my mammy and pappy and brothers was made fiel' slaves.

"Our marster, Dr. Wortham, sho' was a fine doctor. He never whip us. De young missus learned us our A B C's 'cause dere was no school for de slaves. Dere wasn' no church on de plantation, but us all went 'casionally to a big log cabin and camp shed. Sometime a white would preach and sometime a cullud preacher.

"I only 'member one slave who ran away. He was so worthless, he came back when he got ready. He wasn' punished, 'cause he wasn' mean, just lazy. I never saw no jail for slaves and never saw any whipped. We allus had from Friday noon to Monday mornin' off.

"On Christmas, the white folks allus give us presents and plenty to eat, and us allus had a big dance five or six time a year. Dr. Wortham lived in a great big log house made from cedar logs.

"One day, I seen a lot of men and I asked de missus what dey was doin'. She tol' me dey come to fit in de war. De war got so bad dat Mr. Bob tol' us we was all gwine to Texas. Us all started out on Christmas Day of de firs' year of Lincoln's war. We went in ox wagons and us had mules to ride.

"On de trip to Texas, one evenin' a big storm come up and Mr. Bob, he asked a man to let us use a big, empty house. Dey put me by de door to sleep 'cause I was de lightes' sleeper. Some time in de night, I woked up and dere stood de bigges' haint I ever saw. He was ten feet high and had on a big beaver coat. I hollers to my pappy, 'Pappy, wake up, dere's a haint.' Nex' mornin' we got up and dey was nothin' outta place. No, ma'am, we didn' cotch de haint, a haint jus' can't be cotched.

"Nex' mornin' we started agin on our journey, and some time in March we reach Texas. They took us all 'cross de Brazos on a ferryboat, jus' 'bout where de 'spension bridge is now.

"De doctor took us all on de farm on de other side of where Bosque is now. On de farm us raised all kinds vegetables and grain and sugar cane to make sorghum, but no cotton. We all lived in one and two room log cabins, made out of cedar posts. Us didn' make any money for ourselves, but us had plenty of hog meat, beef, butter, milk, cornbread and vegetables to eat, lots mo' dan us have dese days. Us did all de cookin' in de fireplaces. Us sho' did have plenty of possum, and rabbit, and us cotched lots of fish outta de Bosque River.

"De women slaves, eleven of us, had our own gardens and us spun all our own clothes. In de summer us all wore cotton stripe and in de winter, linsey dresses. On Sunday us had lawn dresses and us sho' did come out looking choicesome.

"Dr. Wortham had Si for an overseer. It was a big farm and had forty or fifty slaves to work it. Us got up 'bout four in de mornin' and ate breakfas' 'bout nine o'clock. All de slaves had to work from sun to sun, and when us was sick, de marster treated us.

"When I was 'bout 16, I married William Wright. He was bo'n a slave near Rapid Pass, Kentucky. When he was eight year old, his family's owner died, and he went to the daughter, Mrs. Richard Mason, on Black River, in Louisiana, as "heir property." He was raised dere, but when he's freed he comes to Texas and works for Ganey Mason, seven mile east of Waco. He's 105 year old now and you cain't ha'dly unnerstan' what he's talkin' 'bout. We was married on the 23d day of December, in 1869. Will and me sho' did have a fine weddin'. De women cooked for three days and we danced and ate. My weddin' dress was elegant. It was white lawn with blue ribbons. Will and me had 12 chillen and raised 9, and us has 14 grandchildren.

"Will and me has been married 'bout 75 year and is still married. It's disrespectful how de young folks treats marriage nowadays.

"Ten year after our chillen's growed, we swaps what land we has for dis little house, but we had to pay some money, too. Will was more'n 90 years old and I was eighty some years old, but we got this house and we is happy. We can sit under that big china-berry tree in de fron' yard and look at de big trees over dere on Waco Creek, and one of our sons lives with us."

SALLIE WROE

Sallie Wroe, 81, was born a slave on Mike Burdette's plantation near Austin. Her parents were field workers. In 1874 Sallie married John Wroe and they raised eleven children. Sallie owns a small farm on the outskirts of Austin. One of her daughters lives with her.

"Befo' I's married, I's Sallie Burdette. De white folks tell me I's born eighty-one years ago. I reckon I's dat old. I know I's born on Massa Mike Burdette's cotton plantation at Burdette Prairie, right close to Austin, and mammy's name was Het Burdette. She chopped and picked cotton and been dead long time. John Burdette was my pappy and he was jes' a reg'lar fieldman, too. Pappy been dead, mercy, so long!

"Massa Burdette had a overseer and he sho' rough. I think his name must be Debbil, he so rough. My sister, Mollie, was weaver at de loom, and iffen she didn't git out 'nough for de day she am tied up in sittin' form and whipped hard. She had stripes all over de shoulders.

"Dere was a whole row of log cabins close to de big house and de roofs was made of clapboards. It didn't rain in none. De only openin' was de door, no windows. Dere was mud and stick chimnies and a dirt floor. It wasn't no better dan a corncrib but purty warm in winter, 'cause de holes chinked with mud.

"Massa Burdette 'low us nigger chillen come to de big house at night and his chillen larn us to read. Dey had blue-back spellers, but I didn't cotch on much and can't read or write now.

"Pappy a purty good man, 'siderin' he a slave man. One day pappy and Uncle Paul and Uncle Andy and Uncle Joe was takin' bales of cotton on ox wagons down to de Rio Grande. Each man was drivin' a ox wagon down to Brownsville, where dey was to wait to meet Massa Burdette. But pappy and de others left de wagons 'long de river bank and rolled a bale of cotton in de river and all four of dem gits on dat bale and rows with sticks 'cross over into Mexico. Dis was durin' de war. Pappy come back to us after freedom and say he done git 'long fine with Mexico. He larnt to talk jes' like dem.

Sallie Wroe

"Me and mammy stays on at Massa Burdette's place de whole time pappy am gone. It was on June 19 we was made free and Massa Burdette say iffen we stays on his place and gather de crops, he give each of us a free eggnog. We ain't never got no eggnog befo' so it sound purty good and we stays and gathers de crops. But dat eggnog made me sick.

"My cousin Mitchell come and got us and brung us to Chapel Hill. He done rent him a farm dere and looks out for us till pappy comes back. He brung some money back from Mexico and taken us all to Brenham and buyed us some clothes. Den he moved us up to Austin and done any work he could git. I stayed home till 1874 and den married John Wroe, and he rented land and farmed and died in 1927.

"We raises eleven chillen and dey all good and 'haved. All my grandchillen calls me 'Big Mama,' but I's so li'l now dey ought to call me 'Li'l Mama.' I owns dis li'l farm. John saved 'nough money to buy it befo' he died. I gits a li'l pension and my daughter works and when she's workin' my grandchil' takes care of me."

FANNIE YARBROUGH

Fannie Yarbrough, blind and bedridden, was born a slave of the McKinney family, near Egypt, Kaufman Co., Texas. She was about six when the Civil War started. At that time her job was to herd sheep. After "freedom" she, her mother and sister, stayed with the McKinney's for a time. Fannie married Green Yarbrough in Hunt Co., Texas and they now live in a little cabin at 843 Plum St., Abilene, Texas.

"Ole Marster had a world of sheeps. Every day we take dem sheeps and watch 'em. The wolves was mean. We'd git to playin', all us little niggers, and forgit them sheeps and nex' thing you know an old wolf would have himse'f a sheep.

"Sometimes we'd keep playin' so late it was dark 'fore we knowed it and we'd start runnin' them sheeps home. Ol' Marster would be at de big gate to let us in. He says, 'Now, chillen, you didn' git back with all the sheep.' We'd say, 'Ol' wolf got 'em.' But he knowed ol' wolf didn' get all de ones missin' and he'd say, 'You're storyin'. Then purty soon some of the little stray ones come home. Then he knowed we'd run the sheep home and he'd say, 'I 'spose I'll have to whip you,' but he never did. Those were sweet times! Ol' Marster was so good, and he give us more to eat than you ever saw. Hog meat every day and sweet 'tatoes so big we'd have to cut 'em with an ax.

After we et our supper, we had to spin a broach of thread every night 'fore we went to bed. I larned all 'bout spinnin' and weavin' when I was little and by time I's 10 I'd make pretty striped cloth.

"How we played and played! On Sundays we'd strike out for the big woods and we'd gather our dresses full of hickory nuts, walnuts and berries and a sour apple called 'maypop.' We'd kill snakes and dance and sing that ol' song 'bout, 'Hurrah! Mister Bluecoat, Toodle-O.' 'O, Dat Lady's Beatin' You.' It meant his pardner was beatin' him dancin.'

"I was jes' lyin' here dreamin' 'bout how we use to go to the woods every spring and dig the maypop roots, then bring 'em home and wash 'em good and dry 'em—but, mind you, not in the sun—then all us chillen would sit 'round and poun' dem roots, tied up in little bags of coarse cloth, till it was powder. Then we'd take a little flour and jes' enough water to make it stick, and we'd make pills to take when we got sick. And work you? Lawd a'mighty! When we took dat stuff we had to keep tendin' to de dress tail!

"We went over to Flat Rock to church and de singin' was gran.' All day long we'd be at preachin' and singin'. Singin' dat good ol' spiritual song 'bout, 'You shan't be Slaves no More, since Christ have made you free.' I lay here yes'day and heared all them foolish songs and jubilee songs that comes over the radio, and den some of them ol' time spirituals come and it jes' made me feel like I was in ol' times.

"I went back every year to see my ol' marster, as long as he lived. Now it won' be long till I sees him agin, some day."

United States. Work Projects Administration

LITT YOUNG

Litt Young was born in 1850, in Vicksburg, Miss., a slave of Martha Gibbs, on whose property the old battleground at Vicksburg was located. Litt was freed in 1865, in Vicksburg, and was refugeed by his owner to Harrison Co., Texas. He was freed again on June 19, 1866, and found work as a sawmill hand, a tie cutter and a woodcutter during the construction of the Texas & Pacific Railroad from Marshall to Texarkana. The remainder of his life, with the exception of five years on a farm, has been spent as a section hand. Litt lives alone on the Powder Mill Road, two and a half miles north of Marshall, and is supported by a $12.00 monthly pension from the government.

"I's born in 1850 in Vicksburg, and belonged to Missy Martha Gibbs. Her place was on Warner Bayou and the old battlefield was right there in her field. She had two husbands, one named Hockley and he died of yellow fever. Then she marries a Dr. Gibbs, what was a Yankee, but she didn't know it till after the war.

"Massa Hockley bought my daddy from a nigger trader up north somewheres, but my mammy allus belonged to the Gibbs family. I had a sister and two brothers, but the Gibbs sold them to the Simmons and I never seed 'em any more.

"Old Missy Gibbs had so many niggers she had to have lots of quarters. They was good houses, weatherboarded with cypress and had brick chimneys. We'd pull green grass and bury it awhile, then bile it to make mattresses. That made it black like in auto seats. Missy was a big, rich Irishwoman and not scared of no man. She lived in a big, fine house, and buckled on two guns and come out to the place most every morning. She out-cussed a man when things didn't go right. A yellow man driv her down in a two-horse avalanche. She had a white man for overseer what live in a good house close to the quarters. It was whitewashed and had glass windows. She built a nice church with glass windows and a brass cupola for the blacks and a yellow man preached to us. She had him preach how we was to obey our master and missy if we want to go to Heaven, but when she wasn't there, he come out with straight preachin' from the Bible.

"Good gracious, what we had to eat. They give us plenty, turnip greens and hog-jowl and peas and cornbread and milk by the barrels. Old women what was too old to work in the field done the cookin' and tended the babies. They cooked the cornbread in a oven and browned it like cake. When they pulled it out, all the chillen was standin' round, smackin' they lips. Every Christmas us got a set white lowell clothes and a pair brogan shoes and they done us the whole year, or us go naked.

"When that big bell rung at four o'clock you'd better get up, 'cause the overseer was standin' there with a whippin' strap if you was late. My daddy got a sleepin' most every morning for oversleeping. Them mules was standin' in the field at daylight, waitin' to see how to plow a straight furrow. If a nigger was a 500 pound cotton picker and didn't weigh up that much at night, that was not gittin' his task and he got a whipping. The last weighin' was done by lightin' a candle to see the scales.

"Us have small dances Saturday nights and ring plays and banjo and fiddle playin' and knockin' bones. There was fiddles make from gourds and banjoes from sheep hides. I 'member one song, 'Coffee grows on white oak trees, River flows with brandy-o.' That song was started in Vicksburg by the Yankee soldiers when they left to go home, 'cause they so glad war was over.

"Missy have a big, steam sawmill there on Warner Bayou, where the steamboats come up for lumber. It was right there where the bayou empties in the Mississippi. I 'member seein' one man sold there at the sawmill. He hit his massa in the head with a singletree and kilt him and they's fixin' to hang him, but a man promised to buy him if he'd promise to be good. He give $500 for him.

"Dr. Gibbs was a powerful man in Vicksburg. He was the 'casion of them Yanks takin' 'vantage of Vicksburg like they done. 'Fore the war he'd say to missy, 'Darling, you oughtn't whip them poor, black folks so hard. They is gwine be free like us some day.' Missy say, 'Shut up. Sometimes I 'lieve you is a Yankee, anyway.'

"Some folks say Dr. Gibbs was workin' for the North all the time 'fore the war, and when he doctored for them durin' the war, they say they knowed it. The 'Federates have a big camp there at Vicksburg and cut a big ditch out at the edge of town. Some say Gen. Grant was knowin' all how it was fixed, and that Dr. Gibbs let him know.

"The Yankees stole the march on the 'Federates and

waited till they come out the ditch and mowed 'em down. The 'Federates didn't have no chance, 'cause they didn't have no cannon, jus' cap and ball rifles. The main fight started 'bout four in the morning and held on till 'bout ten. Dead soldiers was layin' thick on the ground by then. After the fight, the Yanks cut the buttons off the coats of them that was kilt.

"I seed the Yankee gunboats when they come to Vicksburg. All us niggers went down to the river to see 'em. They told us to git plumb away, 'cause they didn't know which way they was gwine to shoot. Gen. Grant come to Vicksburg and he blowed a horn and them cannons began to shoot and jus' kept shootin'. When the Yankees come to Vicksburg, a big, red flag was flyin' over the town. Five or six hours after them cannons started shootin' they pulled it down and histed a big, white one. We saw it from the quarters.

Litt Young

"After surrender the Yanks arrested my old missy and brought her out to the farm and locked her up in the black folks church. She had a guard day and night. They fed her hard-tack and water for three days 'fore they turned her a-loose. Then she freed all her niggers. 'Bout that time

Massa Gibbs run out of corn to feed he stock and he took my daddy and a bunch of niggers and left to buy a boatload of corn. Missy seized a bunch us niggers and starts to Texas. She had Irishmen guards, with rifles, to keep us from runnin' 'way. She left with ten six-mule teams and one ox cook wagon. Them what was able walked all the way from Vicksburg to Texas. We camped at night and they tied the men to trees. We couldn't git away with them Irishmen havin' rifles. Black folks nat'rally scart of guns, anyway. Missy finally locates 'bout three miles from Marshall and we made her first crop and on June 19th, the next year after 'mancipation, she sot us free.

"Dr. Gibbs followed her to Texas. He said the Yanks captured his niggers and took his load of corn as they was comin' down the Tennessee River, where it jines the Mississippi. Me and mammy stayed in Texas, and never did see daddy 'gain. When us freed the last time us come to Marshall and I works in a grist mill and shingle mill. I cut ties for 15¢ apiece. I cut wood for the first engines and they paid me $1.25 a cord. I got where I cut three cords a day. I helped clear all the land where Texarkana is now. When the railroads quit using wood, I worked as section hand for $1.25 a day. I farmed five years and never made a cent and went back to the railroad.

"I marries in Marshall so long ago I done forgot. I raises six gals and has three sets grandchillen. They's all livin' 'cept one. Since my wife died and I's too ailing to work, I's been kept by the pension.

"They had provost law in Marshall when us come to Texas. I allus voted when they let us. These young niggers ain't like what us was. Penitentiaries was made for the white folks, but the young niggers is keepin' 'em full."

LOUIS YOUNG

Louis Young, 88, was born a slave of Hampton Atkinson, on a small farm in Phillips County, Arkansas. When Louis was twelve, his master sold him and his mother to Tom Young, who took them to Robinson Co., Texas. Louis now lives at 5523 Bonnell St., Fort Worth, Tex.

"Mammy done put my age in de Bible and I'm eighty-eight years old now. I'm born in 1849. But I can git round. Course, I can't work now, but, shucks, I done my share of work already. I works from time I'm eight years old till I'm eighty past, and I'd be workin' yit if de rheumatis' misery didn't git me in de arms and legs. It make me stiff, so I can't walk good.

"Yes, suh, I starts to work when eight on dat plantation where I'm born. Dat in Arkansaw, and Massa Hampton own me and my mammy and eight other niggers. My pappy am somewhere, but I don't know where or nothin' 'bout him.

"Us all work from light to dark and Sunday, too. I don't know what Sunday am till us come to Texas, and dances and good things, I don't know nothin' 'bout dem till us come to Texas. Massa Hampton, he am long on de work and short on de rations, what he measure out for de week. Seven pounds meat and one peck meal and one quart 'lasses, and no more for de week. If us run out, us am out, dat's all.

"One day us gits sold to Massa Tom Young. He feels mammy's muscles and looks on her for marks of de whip. Massa Young say he give $700, but Massa Hampton say no, he want $1,000. He say, 'Yous takin' dem to Texas, where dey sho' to be slaves, 'spite de war.'

"Finally Massa Young gives $900 for us and off us go to Texas. Dat in 1861, de fall de year, and it am three teams mules and three teams oxen hitch to wagons full of farm things and rations and sich. Us on de road more'n three weeks, maybe a month, befo' us git to Robinson County.

"When us git dere, de work am buildin' de cabins and house and den clear de land, and by Spring, us ready to put in de crops, de corn and cotton. Massa Young am good and give us plenty to eat. He has 'bout twenty slaves and us works reason'ble, and has good time 'pared with befo'. On Saturday night it am dancin' and music and singin', and us never heared of sich befo'.

"One day Massa Young call us to de house and tell us he don't own us no more, and say us can stay and he pay us some money, if us wants. He ask mammy to stay and cook and she does, but I'm strongheaded and runs off to Calvert and goes to work for Massa Brown, and dere I stays till I'm growed. He paid me $10.00 de month and den $15.00.

"When I's twenty-five I marries Addie Easter and us have no chillen and she dies ten years after. Den I drifts 'round, workin' here and yonder and in 1890 I marries dat woman settin' right dere. Den I rents de farm and if de crops am good, de prices am bad, and if de prices am good, de crops am bad. So it go and us lives, and not too good, at dat. I quits in 1925 and comes to Fort Worth and piddles at odd jobs till my rheumatis' git so bad five years ago.

"I done forgit to tell you 'bout de Klux. Dem debbils causes lots of trouble. Dey done de dirty work at night, come and took folks out and whip dem.

Louis Young

"Some cullud folks am whip so hard dey in bed sev'ral weeks and I knowed some hanged by dey thumbs. Maybe some dem cullud folks gits out dere places, but mostest dem I knows gits whip for nothin'. It jus' de orneriness dem Klux. It so bad de cullud folks 'fraid to sleep in dey house or have parties or nothin' after dark. Dey starts for de woods or ditches and sleeps dere. It git so dey can't work for not sleepin', from fear of dem Klux. Den de white folks takes a hand and sojers am brung and dey puts de stop to dem debbils.

"'Bout de livin' now, us jus' can't make it. Us lives on what de pension am and dat $30.00 de month, and it mighty close us has to live to git by on sich. I thinks of Massa Young, and us live better den dan now.

"I never votes, 'cause I can't read and dat make troublement for me to vote. How I gwine make de ticket for dis and dat? For dem what can read, dey can vote."

TESHAN YOUNG

Teshan Young, 86, was born a slave to Buckner Scott, who owned a plantation in Harrison County, Texas, and had over one hundred slaves. Teshan married Moses Young in 1867 and lived near her old home until 1915, when she moved to Fort Worth. She lives in a negro settlement on the outskirts of Stop Six, a suburb of Fort Worth.

"I'se 86 years ole. Bo'n in Harrison County, Texas. Marster Scott owned me and my parents, one brudder and three sisters. Marster never sold any of we'uns, so dere was no separation of de family long's we lived on de Marster's place. He had awful big plantation, 'bout seven miles long.

"On dat plantation de Marster have everything. Hims have de gin and de mill for to grind de meal and feed, de big blacksmith shop and dere was a house whar dey spins de yarn and makes de cloth, de shoes and sich. He have 'bout 30 quarters for de cullud folks back of him's house, and dere am a house for de nursery, wid a big yard dat have swings and sich for de cullud chillens.

"Each cullud family have de cabin for themself. De cabins have bunks for sleeping', fireplace for to cook, bench for to set on—but dat's all de furniture. Marster Scott feeds all us niggers good. We'uns have beans, peas, milk, vegetables, 'lasses and plenty of meat. De marster have hawgs on top of hawgs on dat place, for to make de meat.

"We'uns have all de clothes dat we'uns need for to keep warm. De marster says, 'De nigger mus' have plenty of food and keep wan for to work good. How many hours we'uns work? Dat depen's on de time of de year it am. When its time for de hoein' or de pickin' of de cotton, dey work late. 'Twarn't sich long hours udder times. But de marster makes de cullud folks work and whips 'em when dey don'. I'se 'member one slave dat gits whipped so bad hims never gits up, hims died. We'uns chillens would go roun' whar hims was and look at 'im. De Marster lets we'uns do dat.

"Yes, suh, dey whupped pow'ful hard sometimes. My mammy gits whupped one time 'cause she come from de fiel' for to nuss her baby, and once for de cause she don' keep up her row in de fiel'. My pappy gits shoot in de shoulder by de overseer, 'cause hims runs from de whuppin.' 'Twas dis way, de overseer says, 'Come here, I'se gwine whup you for not workin' like I says.' Dere was a fence dere and my pappy runs for dat and am crawlin' over it when de overseer shoots.

"I'se 'bout 10 year ole when de war starts. It makes no diff'rence, dat I'se 'members, 'cept de Marster jines de army. I'se tend to all de cullud chillen while dey mammies workin' in de fiel'. De Marster am sho' particular 'bout dem chillen. He feeds 'em well, mush, milk, bread, 'lasses, vegetables and sich. De food am put in de long bowl, like de trough. De chillen have wooden spoons and we'uns line dem 'long de bowl. Den de fun starts. I'se have de long switch and keeps walkin' back and forth to make dem debils behave. De Marster comes in sometimes and hims laugh at dem, dey so funny.

"After I'se gits married, I'se has 13 chillen of my own. I'se never calls de doctor for my chillen. I'se goes in de woods and gits de plants and de herbs. For de stomach misery I'se uses de red petals, boils dat and takes de juice. For de cold I'se takes de Kalemas Root, boils dat and takes de juice.

Teshan Young

"When de chores am done on Sunday or Christmas, we'uns can have de music, dance and singin'. We'uns have some good ole times. De songs am de ole timers, sich as Swannee River, Ole Black Joe and dere am de fiddles and banjos dat dey play. We'uns sho' cel'brate on Christmas. De women all cooks cakes and cookies and sich. De men saves all de bladders from de hawgs dey kill, blows 'em full of air and lets 'em dry. De young'uns puts dem on sticks and holds 'em over a fire in de yard. Dat makes 'em bust and dey goes 'bang' jus' like a gun. Dat was de fireworks.

"Marster comes back from de war widout gettin' hurt. At de time freedom comes, some cullud folks stays on and works for money. 'Twas de fust money dey ever had, and dey don' know what to do wid it and what its worth. Some of dem are still on dat lan'! Dey rents or have bought. My brudder lives dere, jus' a few yards from de ole quarters. My pappy worked for ole Marster till he died. I'se stays wid him till I marries.

"I'se married in a cullud church and I'se have a pretty pink dress and hat. My husban' have hims own farm, part of de ole plantation. We finally buys it from de Marster. In 1902 my husban' dies and I'se stays dere till 1915. Den I'se comes to Fort Worth. I'se still missin' some but I'se gettin' de pension of nine dollars a month. Dat sho' helps out."

Transcriber's Note

Original spelling has been maintained; e.g. "*stob*—a short straight piece of wood, such as a stake" (American Heritage Dictionary).—The Works Progress Administration was renamed during 1939 as the Work Projects Administration (WPA).

www.ingramcontent.com/pod-product-compliance
Lightning Source LLC
Chambersburg PA
CBHW071649160426
43195CB00012B/1407